Inhabited Silence
in Qualitative Research

Studies in the
Postmodern Theory of Education

Joe L. Kincheloe and Shirley R. Steinberg
General Editors

Vol. 318

PETER LANG
New York • Washington, D.C./Baltimore • Bern
Frankfurt am Main • Berlin • Brussels • Vienna • Oxford

Lisa A. Mazzei

Inhabited Silence
in Qualitative Research

Putting Poststructural Theory to Work

PETER LANG
New York • Washington, D.C./Baltimore • Bern
Frankfurt am Main • Berlin • Brussels • Vienna • Oxford

Library of Congress Cataloging-in-Publication Data

Mazzei, Lisa A.
Inhabited silence in qualitative research: putting poststructural theory to work /
Lisa A. Mazzei.
p. cm. — (Counterpoints: studies in the postmodern theory of education; vol. 318)
Includes bibliographical references and index.
1. Education—Research—Philosophy. 2. Silence. 3. Qualitative research.
4. Poststructuralism. I. Title.
LB1028.M354   370.7'2—dc22   2006037195
ISBN 978-0-8204-8876-9
ISSN 1058-1634

Bibliographic information published by **Die Deutsche Bibliothek**.
Die Deutsche Bibliothek lists this publication in the "Deutsche
Nationalbibliografie"; detailed bibliographic data is available
on the Internet at http://dnb.ddb.de/.

Cover image: Silhouettes in memory of Jews deported from the Grunewald Station,
sculpture by Karol Broniatowski. Photograph by Roy Winkelman,
© Florida Center for Instructional Technology, University of South Florida

The paper in this book meets the guidelines for permanence and durability
of the Committee on Production Guidelines for Book Longevity
of the Council of Library Resources.

© 2007 Peter Lang Publishing, Inc., New York
29 Broadway, 18th floor, New York, NY 10006
www.peterlang.com

for phillip

who brought poetry into my life

What I don't want to say or cannot, the unsaid, the forbidden, what is passed over in silence, what is separated off...—all these should be interpreted.

—Jacques Derrida, *Of Hospitality*

TABLE OF CONTENTS

PREFACE

What is haunting the discourse that betrays what is being said here?

—Dan Miller[1]

How important is silence? This question haunts me as surely as the creaks and groans of an old house at three o'clock in the morning. If silence is important, what is its significance in the records of research? There is the silence of the non-spoken that we can hear as idle emptiness or as "speech" filled with "unspeakable content." Silence can be the haunting presence, the seemingly unintelligible element in our research that goes unnamed, unnoticed, or perhaps, even ignored. Silence, it would seem, is that specter that rattles around in the dark, underneath, in between, in front of our acts of discourse to subvert, conflict, and at times to make clear to us our intentions and possibly our actions.

In the context of qualitative research, specifically qualitative research that concerns itself with an analysis of speech and conversations, *good* methodologists are taught to organize what they have "*seen, heard, and read* [emphasis mine]" (Glesne, 1999, p. 130) in order to make sense of what they have learned. Good methodologists are taught to focus on and analyze what participants talk about, what they tell us, what they describe, what they recount. Good methodologists are carefully, carefully taught to be attentive to their field notes and transcription data, and if nothing is said, to turn their attention to another day, another conversation, another participant. What good methodologists are not taught is how to hear silence, to listen to the import in the discourse that weaves its way in and through speech and conversations with barely a whisper.

Thus my aim in this book is to gesture toward a methodology that takes seriously the importance of silence in discourse-based qualitative research. I am proposing a consideration of silence not as a lack, an absence, or negation but rather as an important and even vital aspect of the fabric of discourse. My theorizing of silence suggests that we consider silence as a part of the whole, the relevant speech act "spoken" beneath the surface, in the interstices, around the corners of our ordinary perceptual frames, enabling a more careful reading (listening) of what our participants are in fact saying, even when they are not speaking. Furthermore, I want to move our attention toward a consideration of silence in a fashion similar to the way that Heidegger considers the "nothing," not as an absence or a void, but as something experienced or encountered. The unspoken that when heard "shakes us loose from our preoccupations with 'what is'" (Caputo, 1986, p. 19).[2]

Of course, in order to be shaken loose, we must develop a methodology that helps us listen to the voice of silence and also develop a theoretical understanding of silences as *meaning full* in qualitative research. Such purposeful attentiveness to the inhabited silences in discourse-based research will serve to provide a more textured and nuanced understanding than can be obtained when simply focusing on the words that are spoken. Instead of being content with that which is outwardly discernible, we can pursue that which is found in the muffled words not spoken or silent. An important aspect of a methodology used to achieve this sifting of layers employs a deconstructive reading of the data. Engaging in a deconstructive reading leads to a greater awareness of the competing tendencies in the data (text), not in an effort to deny the dominating tendencies that are present, but to consider what else may be "echoing" as muffled subtext. It is out of this fog of the muffled subtext, the unspoken, the intentionally silenced, that the meaning and purpose of silence in discourse-based qualitative research can be rendered in its importance through bringing into play a deconstructive methodology.

In the conversations in which qualitative researchers engage, silences often occur, particularly when researchers work at understanding culturally sensitive subjects such as race, ethnicity, and sexuality and their effect in the educational milieu. How do we take seriously this silence or recognize its effects if it is marked only by an absence of voice? Informed by poststructural theory, I propose that qualitative researchers not dismiss silence as an omission or absence of empirical materials, but rather engage the silences as meaningful and purposeful. As Caputo suggests, this awareness will not only shake us loose from our preoccupations with what is, but it will also release the specters of silence to be heard in the stories yet untold. Perhaps then we will begin to recognize the silence haunting the discourse that betrays what is being said here.

ACKNOWLEDGMENTS

Lone scholar I am not, and for the support, encouragement, and help in my fulfilment of this project, I owe special thanks to many. Without Phillip, who for many years now has been my most enthusiastic and unfailing editor, partner, sounding board, and cook, I would not have had the time nor the discipline to pursue the dream. Patti Lather, who prompted me to get lost from our first meeting and who sent me on my way. Jack Caputo, for inspiring me through his writings, for sharing the generosity of his spirit and intellect, and for opening up the possibility of the *impossible*. Cynthia Tyson, for being my friend, teacher, and *sister*. Mary Todd for understanding the desire and demands of such a project and for supporting me in so many ways in her role as my VPAA and colleague. Ohio Dominican University for supporting the sabbatical and travel to Syracuse University that permitted the space and exchange for the articulation of my ideas. Harry Torrance, Director of the Education and Social Research Institute at Manchester Metropolitan University for granting me the time and support to finish this project after my arrival in England. Roy Winkelman and the Florida Center for Instructional Technology for providing the photograph used for the cover. Sophie Appel of Peter Lang for her wonderful assistance throughout the production process. Karen Longbrake and Debbie Guru for rewarding me with good wine and friendship and for checking on my progress even after I moved away. My parents Frank & Charmaine, and the rest of my family, for encouraging me from the day I was born. My favorite felines, Giugno & Ionious—my companions from the beginning of this journey—and Lucia & Artemisia—who taught me to listen. And especially to my readers without whom I wouldn't have been able to make my silences audible: Phillip Prince, Jeremy Glazier, Alisha Waller, Ian Stronach, Maggie MacLure and Helen Colley.

Permission was provided by the following journals to use previously published material. While the articles are not reproduced in their original form, they serve as the basis for several chapters.

CHAPTER 1
The Voice of Silence

> We are going to talk about silence—an impossible task.
>
> —John Caputo[1]

What Does It Mean to Mean?

My pursuit in this methodological searching is to access the meaning to be found in the silences haunting our encounters in the field. And at its heart it is a "troubling" of the attachment to the ways in which we conceive of and consider meaning, data and speech.[2] It is a desire to pursue that which defies interpretation rather than that which is self-evident, to focus attention on what is dimly seen, faintly heard, tentatively voiced beyond the univocal interpretations clearly seen, forcefully heard and strongly voiced. Jacques Derrida (1994/1993) reminds us that "If the readability of a legacy were given, natural, transparent, univocal, if it did not call for and at the same time defy interpretation, we would never have anything to inherit from it" (p. 16).

Within this inheritance as qualitative researchers is a valorizing of speech, voices heard and recorded. What if in an acceptance of this inheritance we were to engage in a troubling that resulted in a moving away from a valorizing of speech toward the ways in which this inheritance contains that which defies interpretation, the specters of "silent speech." Might there then be a possibility in the doing of qualitative research, particularly discourse-based research, to trouble our naive notions of "what it means to mean" and to thereby loose ourselves from an attachment to a "thereness" to be found in data (MacLure, 2006)? Instead of an attachment to a "thereness" in the data only to be found in what is audibly voiced, we could pursue an attachment to a "thereness" in the data that is only to be found in a reading that transgresses boundaries, that is an articulation of the disjointure between presence and absence, between what is spoken with words and between words, between what absents itself and what presents itself, between what is transparent and what is veiled. It is this "thereness," this absent presence, this specter of silence that defies containment and furtively slips through our "way of knowing" that is of concern here.

This other "way of knowing," if I can put it that way, does not exclude a continued rigorous attention to received theory and method in the doing of qualitative research, rather it overturns and overflows its received idea(s) (Derrida, 1994, p. 34) and strives to put to work a poststructural theoretical approach. Of course mine is not the first attempt to engage poststructural theory in the doing of qualitative research (see, for example, Lather, 1993, 2004; Lather & Smithies, 1997; Peters & Burbules, 2004; St. Pierre & Pillow, 2000; Scheurich, 1997; Stronach & MacLure, 1997); however, I believe that my approach differs in that through the use of poststructural theory, particularly deconstruction, a new data set is named and "listened to," one previously lacking in the methodological literature, namely silence. Informed by poststructural theory, I propose that qualitative researchers not dismiss silence as an omission or absence of empirical materials, but rather engage the silences as *meaning full* and *purpose full*.

Thereness in Nothingness?

"How do you do Nothing?" asked Pooh, after he had wondered for a long time.

"Well, it's when people call out at you just as you're going off to do it, What are you going to do, Christopher Robin, and you say Oh, nothing, and then you go and do it."

"Oh, I see," said Pooh.

"This is a nothing sort of thing that we're doing now."
"Oh, I see," said Pooh again.

"It means just going along, listening to all the things you can't hear, and not bothering."

"Oh!" said Pooh.

Chapter X of *The House at Pooh Corner*
—AA Milne

Several years ago the beginnings of my work with white teachers prompted my incipient questioning of the "thereness" to be found in the spoken and printed words of the transcript. Like Christopher Robin, I began listening to all the things I couldn't hear, and instead of "not bothering" I was *extremely bothered*! Were there things that I could hear, but had previously not considered because I had not bothered? Had I not bothered because I was too focused on what was at hand and not enough on the "out of hand?"

The research project in which I was engaged was a qualitative research study with a group of white teachers in an urban school district. I met this group of teachers when we were all enrolled in a graduate course exploring multicultural education. The course, made up of approximately 50 public school teachers, was sponsored by their school district and taught through the university. Following the course, five teachers from the class consisting of four women and one man, responded to my initiative to engage in a continuing dialogue and exploration developed around issues generated by the course. Our agreed purpose was to further investigate multicultural topics that the course had failed to probe sufficiently and to attend to questions that the course had raised but not adequately addressed. As co-participants in this project, we each brought the experience of being a white teacher and the shared educational experience of participation in the above mentioned graduate course. Although the teachers in this study were clearly "research subjects," they were not passive participants to which a litany of one-way questions was directed. They were encouraged to bring their own agendas and unresolved issues to each group session and did so. The process was as much about "meaning-making" as it was about "mining" information (Holstein & Gubrium, 1995).

My intent, in fact, was to examine the affect of the racial positioning of white teachers in a non-white environment on their perception of themselves in relation to their students and concurrently how this affected their curricular and pedagogical decisions. Additionally, how did a stated racial positioning inform their experience as teachers in settings in which they were in the minority, i.e., where whiteness was made visible only by its absence in the surrounding milieu.[3]

In the early stages of sifting through the conversations with these teachers, what emerged was their reticence to engage questions of race and culture in education, especially when these questions shifted the attention to them as white. I found that this group of teachers did not see themselves as having a racial identity, or at least not one that they saw as "visible," and certainly not one they could comfortably articulate. In recounting her work with white preservice teachers, Pearl Rosenberg (1997) observed, "For some, their identity as white people only takes shape *in relation* to others" (p. 80). Consistent with Rosenberg's experience, the teachers in my study when discussing multicultural education and race often focused on those who were not like themselves, non-whites in their environment, without consideration of themselves as part of a racial discourse. The unconscious, or perhaps conscious, result was to continue to see their world through a veil of whiteness. They were not seeing themselves, nor were they seeing themselves seen (Cixous, 2001).

This notion of what we see and don't see as whites and how we define others in relation to ourselves as Other (i.e., different, exotic, inferior) is an important concept in a discussion of whiteness but also in the context of a discussion of silence. Edward Said (1978) challenged readers to question how our writing and thinking about the Other reinscribes our "false" notions about the Other. Further, in *The Mismeasure of Woman*, Carol Tavris (1992) wrote that women are not the better sex, the inferior sex, or the opposite sex, but rather the different sex. Woman can never be normal if man is the measure for woman, for normalcy does not allow for difference. Nonwhite can never be normal if white, and particularly white middle class, is the measure for normal. Silence can never receive a "hearing" if voiced speech is the measure of what is credible. When we conceive the Other as anyone or anything that is different, we are polarizing the distinctions. If we always use a perceived opposite measure or binary in discussing the Self in relation to the Other (or silence in relation to speech), the danger always exists that polarizing is perpetuated, that the Other is held accountable to a measuring stick of the wrong size.

In *Playing in the Dark*, Toni Morrison (1992) asserted, "My project is an effort to avert the critical gaze from the racial object to the racial subject; from the described and imagined to the describers and imaginers; from the serving to the served" (p. 45). Morrison presented clearly what I anticipated this project would become as the veil of not-seeing-oneself was removed (Cixous, 2001/1998, p. 12). In other words, a shifting of the gaze from Other to Self might enable us to catch a glimpse of our whiteness, rather than the non-whiteness of others, and to ascertain how this shifting of gaze might change our relationship to and with our students and colleagues. We had commenced what was to become a deconstructive project. We were, according to Spivak (1997/1989), embarking on one of Derrida's most scandalous contributions, "to begin with what is very familiar in many radical positions and to take it with the utmost seriousness, with literal seriousness, so that it questions the position (de)constructively as the wholly intimate other" (p. 359).

As we set about this exploration and entered keenly into discussions prompted both by our experience in the multicultural education course and our experience as white teachers in a non-white environment, one aspect of our myopia became immediately apparent. Simply because we were in the minority in our schools did not mean that our whiteness was visible to us; in other words, we still viewed and experienced ourselves as normative and everyone else as Other. We were not yet able to see ourselves reflexively in a way that would achieve a deconstructive rendering of whiteness. We were bound by the Derridian insight of the mother tongue, having been inserted into a history created before we were born (Spivak, 1997/1989, p. 160). As a result, I came to recognize the silences encouraged by that history, ones *purposefully* present in the conversations that we were speaking, but with no history or context with which to give them voice.

Although I had been schooled to work *against* the desire to find truths in the words spoken by my research participants, I was still operating *within* a problematic that gave preference to things seen and heard as understandable and therefore knowable, a traveling through the years of experiences and education that had served to shape and define me (Cixous, 1993, p. 119). It was not possible to stand outside the discursive convention that constituted our understanding of whiteness and the subsequent privilege, but it might be possible as Lather (2000) has stated, to "shift the imaginary" (p. 685) in ways that would allow me to rework and disrupt the very conventions by which I was enabled. These new insights into difference, these reworkings and disruptions, the still-unanswered questions, the silences within the spoken words, prompted a need for me to devise methodological strategies and rationales that would work the *against* with more vigor than the *within,* thereby giving increased attention to the silences existing furtively in the midst of the spoken. Different strategies—theoretical, methodological, and pedagogical—were needed that would enable me to travel a different *soundscape.*

"Derrida advises us to begin *wherever* we are, in the middle of the fix we find ourselves in, in the middle of a text, a phrase, a word, a syllable, with the smallest bit or piece. That at least will enable [us] to get started, not at the beginning, which is to ask too much, but wherever [we are]" (Caputo, 1993, p. 21). Given this advice, I accept the images present from my methodological history, acknowledge the limitations given this historical orientation and am using them to entertain a methodology less bound by their restrictiveness, yet stimulated by the very presence of the enunciative boundaries (Bhabha, 1994). In other words, instead of ignoring or overlooking the absence, I am attempting to exploit the blindness and silence created within the context of my research toward a more fruitful discourse at the edges of its boundaries.

Why Deconstruction?

There is (of course) an epistemological and methodological quandary, a fix, if you will, that I embrace (at least most of the time) but needs now to be "spoken." My encounters with the likes of Derrida, Caputo, Cixous, Lather, Stronach and Mac-Lure (not to mention the specters) leave me uncertain as to the question of what it means to mean and how to mean. This does not mean that I give up on meaning, or research, or understanding. Nor does it mean that I pursue methodological questions because my data have nothing to tell me. It does mean (I think) that I do not naively claim meaning, completeness, or understanding found in the spoken words and printed text. It means that I seek the limits, the boundaries, and the seeming "thereness" of my methodological history in an effort to engage the silent voices of the specters that have much to say in the "not said." It means that I journey into the realm of "fine distinctions, where subtlety, balance [the specters] and keen precision hold sway" (Asimov, 2006, p. D8). It means that I engage methodological strategies that push me beyond the comfortable limits of what is known, what is knowable, and what is accessible. In other words (or without words), it means engaging these specters and their silent speech offered in layers of whispering, breathing, pausing, absenting, such that the question of what it means to mean and how to mean opens itself beyond the received theories or methodologies.

Derrida asserts "every speech act is fundamentally a promise" (Derrida & Caputo, 1997, p. 23). Although these speech acts may manifest themselves both as spoken words and silent breaths, it is important to explore the significance of these silences and the expectation of what is unexpected and sometimes unpredictable—what is yet to come. If we are able to create strategies for listening to the silences such that we are attentive to them when they occur, we will then also be open to the possibility of deconstruction in the surprise of silence. "Deconstruction is set in motion by something that calls upon and addresses us, overtakes (sur-prises) and even overwhelms us, to which we must respond, and so be responsive and responsible. Endlessly" (p. 51). By engaging in a purposeful process for listening to the voices of our participants, and specifically listening to the silences uttered in the breaths and the pauses, we encounter a fascinating discourse often unnoticed that will surprise us and to which we must attend.

A deconstructive practice for listening to silence means that we can take seriously Cixous's description of a shaking up of our received notions. Derrida and Caputo (1997) explain this deconstructive analysis as one that "deprives the present of its prestige and exposes it to something...beyond what is foreseeable from the present" (p. 42). In other words, it presents a methodological approach or strategy with which one can begin to shake up the hierarchy between speech and silence in order that the silence, the always already absent presence, might insert "itself within the interstices of the former, filling holes that are always already there" (Spivak, 1976, p. lxxiv).

A deconstructive practice, then, is a means by which we can engage what constitutes our received history as researchers and particularly what is contained in our methodological history—"the tensions, the contradictions, [and] the heterogeneity within" this history (Derrida & Caputo, 1997, p. 9). "Deconstruction presupposes the intensely cultivated, literate relation to the tradition" (Derrida, 2002, p. 15) necessary in the pursuit of a methodology informed by the tradition but not bound by it. I am not, however, deluded in the use of a deconstructive practice into thinking that this methodological project is without peril, for as Jacques Derrida (quoted by Spivak, 1976) further reminds us, "in the long run a critic cannot [herself] present [her] own vulnerability" (p. lxxxv). However, what is possible is to "analyze the functioning and dysfunctioning" (Derrida & Caputo, 1997, p. 9) present within our received, familiar methodologies concomitant with attention to what Patti Lather (1995) terms a doubling methodology, one that "produces rather than protects" (p. 56), that presents a possibility of the impossible.

Threads of the Text

Writing as editor of *Best American Poetry 1996*, Adrienne Rich suggested that when white poets write of race, "relation-

ships of race and power exist in their poems most often as silence or muffled subtext" (1996, p. 32). Is it then not also possible that these relationships of race and power, as well as
others, exist in the subtexts of empirical materials to be discovered in the unspoken, the inaudible, or the ignored—in the
stories which are silent? I submit that these stories, if listened
to, can tell us much about ourselves, about our research participants, and about our priorities as we interpret discourse-
based empirical materials. I propose that we should therefore
develop strategies for listening to these phenomena differently,
that we should pay increased attention to silent subtexts, to
what is being left out, not said, or intentionally repressed in
our ongoing quest to discover the "truths" within our spoken
stories.

It is this "listening" that I will undertake in the following
chapters. From a discussion of deconstructive theory and
methodology as applied in discourse-based qualitative research
to the putting to work of such an approach, and finally, a look
at the problematic of such an approach, I will show how silence as a strategic element of discourse enables me as a qualitative researcher to attend to silence, not as an omission or
absence of empirical materials, but rather as that to be engaged as *meaning full and purpose full* in our research.

Chapter Two, then, will take up the discussion of how I
conceive of and engage a deconstructive methodology that
permits a different listening in qualitative inquiry. Specifically,
how a deconstructive methodology functions to disrupt the
privileged position of the spoken word in our encounters with
research participants toward a reconceptualized methodology
that irrupts our received notions of "data" and that engages
Derrida's notion of the impossible. In this chapter I rely heavily
on Derrida's concept of the haunting specter as developed in
the first section of *Specters of Marx.* As with the silent words
spoken by our participants, the silent specters beckon and
speak should we have the patience and courage to listen.

Chapter Three expands on the idea of transgressive data
sources as discussed by St. Pierre (1997). Informed by a variety of disciplines (e.g., communication theory, psychotherapy,
literary theory, etc.), as well as the treatment of silence by philosophical writers (e.g., Merleau-Ponty, Heidegger, Derrida, and

Irigaray), the discussion centers on a theorizing of silence as data in the context of qualitative inquiry.

Chapter Four provides a context for the research that I use as a way to both explain and demonstrate the ways in which a poststructural analysis has shifted the problematic not only for the doing of qualitative research, but for understanding the research. It is with Giroux's (1988) explanation of a problematic as being structured by both what is included and what is left out of a worldview that I posit in the doing of qualitative research, specifically discourse-based research, absent in an analysis of conversations with research participants has often been silence. Not because the silences have not been present, but because they have not been recognized. Further, a discussion ensues as to the possibilities present if we begin to view the data and encounters with participants in the field as performances, and how viewing them as such also shifts the problematic, not just in terms of what "counts" but how it is "viewed" and "heard."

In Chapter Five, I present the argument that qualitative researchers not dismiss silence as an omission or absence of empirical materials, but rather engage the silences as meaningful and purposeful. Specifically, this chapter further expounds on the idea of a poetic understanding of silence out of which researchers may explore the significance of silences present in the conversations of discourse-based research as they consider the conversations with research participants as poetic constructions. Chapter Five further serves as a transition chapter between the theoretical grounding of the book and the methodological practices discussed in the subsequent chapters.

Chapter Six provides a specific working example of how I "put poststructural theory to work," specifically the deconstructive writings of Derrida, Caputo, and Cixous, to irrupt efforts at the containment of qualitative research. Specifically, it presents a methodological approach for listening to the "silences" revealed in my conversations with white teachers regarding their racial identity. Those silences, present both in the absence of speech and in speech acts, were "heard" through the use of a deconstructive practice for listening to the conversations. This deconstructive practice allowed the silences to disrupt the tranquil assurance of the spoken word.

Chapter Seven discusses the implications for conducting interviews in pursuit of the silent discourse or of the "interior monologue" (Richardson, 1997). Drawing on the work of theorists such as Scheurich (1997), Kvale (1996, 2006), Richardson (2002), Ochs (1979), and Briggs (1986), a consideration of the methodological implications are developed, not just of the analysis, but also of the asking.

Chapter Eight, the final chapter, proposes a series of undisciplined questions in my attempt to further think the limit of silence in qualitative research and to move toward reflexivities of silence in the practice of qualitative research.

It is hoped that you are intrigued by this uncertain and ambiguous project and that as you listen to the silence, whispers, and specters, you will begin to notice the meanings present in the purposeful silences masking as absence.

CHAPTER 2
A Deconstructive Methodology

> But is this possible? Of course it is not; that is why it is
> the only possible invention of deconstruction.
> —Caputo, 1997, p. 115

Attempting the Impossible

In "Letter to a Japanese Friend," Jacques Derrida (1991) ad-
monishes "Deconstruction is not a method and cannot be
transformed into one," for attempting such may lead to a "do-
mestication" of deconstruction resulting in a "set of rules and
transposable procedures" (p. 273). With that admonition,
might you think me a fool to proffer a deconstructive methodology, and if arrogantly I forge ahead, is such an offering so an-
tithetical to an understanding of deconstruction as to be
"impossible?" In a discussion of this question of method, Richard Beardsworth (cited in Royle, 2000) suggests that "Derrida
is careful to avoid this term ['method'] because it carries con-
notations of a procedural form of judgment. A thinker with a
method has already decided how to proceed, is unable to give
him or herself up to the matter of thought in hand, is a func-
tionary of the criteria which structure his or her conceptual
gestures. For Derrida...this is irresponsibility itself" (p. 4). Is
my pursuit of a deconstructive methodology then not only a
flirting with the impossible but also an act of irresponsibility?
Is it mocking the very process/strategy/method that I seek?
And what exactly is it that I seek? Is it possible?

These questions seem to demand that the only "responsible" course (if that is possible) is to attempt some explication
(with fear and trembling) of a deconstructive methodology as it
might be used in discourse-based research. Let us start with

the "negative." I am not looking for a prescriptive formula for counting data, nor am I attempting to posit a definitive method for recognizing "meaningful" silences. What I am seeking in a deconstructive methodology is the breach, the crevice through which previously unheard data will silently slip to disrupt and destabilize our impressions. Using a deconstructive methodology we move toward a self-questioning and destabilizing strategy that helps us as researchers remain open to "what remains to be thought, with what cannot be thought within the present" (Royle, 2000, p. 7). Such a methodology utilizes an endless quest for the absent presence lurking beneath/under/around/through/within the tangible artifacts that are named and analyzed by qualitative researchers. A deconstructive methodology will serve as a strategy by which qualitative researchers might be present to those elusive specters silently at hand, always waiting to be heard in the layering and spacing of the text (data).

Writing about a deconstructive methodology (especially haunted by Derrida's injunction) is almost as elusive as writing about whiteness, or worse silence. Why pursue a methodology that is continuously self-questioning and always in search of that which is not being said (or at least not *said* in a traditional sense)? My fascination with these *impossible* possibilities, coupled with an attraction to philosophers whose promise of a secret, or of passion, or of the impossible—attainable only as specters—risk leading me down a slippery slope to oblivion or worse, realism. The onus then is to translate this attraction into something that enhances my research—one that produces a methodology that will aid us in exploring the haunting silences present in our research.[1]

Again, when I speak of a deconstructive methodology, I propose not a prescriptive and closed set of procedures, but an essential self-questioning, an opening through which the hidden is encountered, the possible made impossible. In the book *The Prayers & Tears of Jacques Derrida*, John Caputo (1997) has this to say about Derrida's notion of the impossible: "By the impossible Derrida clearly does not mean impossible *stricto sensu*, the simple modal opposite of the possible, but the more-than-possible, the transgression, the chance, the aleatory, the breach, the rupture, the passage to the limits, the *ébranler* and the *solicitation* of the same. The possible is not other, not other enough, not enough at all" (p. 51). In other words, in my pursuit of a deconstructive methodology is the desire for the more-than-possible that presents the possibility of the levels, complexities, and absences in qualitative data analysis not previously considered possible. It is a search for the breach that permits the silent specter to enter our midst. It is a search for a possibility of the impossible (if that is possible).

Derrida (Malibou & Derrida, 2004) further complicates this "possibility" when he states that deconstruction is not a method, but rather "It is what happens" (p. 225). This what happens happens through the process of destabilizing that which craves stability, sameness, hegemony. It is a reading that requires the continuous opening and exploration of the spaces, passion, and silences not yet *deconstructed*. It happens when a search for the previously unheard is allowed to emerge, when the previously thought absent becomes the articulated present. This "not method" happens when the silence is recognized not as an absence, but as a presence, as a critical aspect of the "what happens" when the notion of what *counts* as speech is disrupted and a *more* complete (not complete, but more complete) understanding of what might constitute speech, or the text, or data (in other words the spoken and silent words) is given a hearing.

Perhaps then this pursuit of a deconstructive method is better phrased as the pursuit of a reading or analysis that seeks the excesses, the breaches, the ruptures, while keeping the analysis destabilized enough that something unexpected, something *silent*, something *impossible*, may emerge. Such a method pushes us in a direction as suggested by Heidegger in which we get past the paradoxes and move outside that which is self-evident. Instead of giving up on finding the specific meaning of our reading (as we will be accused), this method or reading becomes *more* responsible, not irresponsible, because it "consists in not providing ready-made responses" (Malibou & Derrida, 2004, p. 239). This reading considers not what the text tends to say, but engages a deconstructive openness to expect, even encourage, another interpretation of the text, a

competing interpretation of the text, an attention to the "echoing" voices in the layers beneath the surface.

What I wish to do can't be done, or at least can't
be finished. As Derrida (2005/2003) himself has stated, if deconstruction stops, there is no more hope for the impossible.
But my pursuit of this method must not be tossed aside due to
the seemingly "impossible" nature of it. Rather, with unbridled
temerity we must move beyond the limits of methodology as
currently understood toward those new limits that result from
our excessive readings.[2]

In *The Mystical Element in Heidegger's Thought*, John
Caputo (1986) writes of Heidegger as "a thinker whose thinking
is conducted at the limits of philosophy" (p. 1). Throughout the
book, Caputo discusses Heidegger's thinking "post philosophy," as he describes Heidegger as wanting to shake loose of
Western philosophy in order "to overcome philosophy and take
up the task of thought" (p. 266). Heidegger speaks of the end of
philosophy as an end to the rationalities and strictures that
limit thought. What he pursues is a transgression of these limits and strictures that open him to the beginning of thought, or
rather, toward the beginning of thought not previously possible
because it was outside or beyond the permissible, seeable,
hearable limits.

A deconstructive methodology, in keeping with this "beyond," represents a methodology that transgresses boundaries,
thrives on excesses and eccentricities, and contests the tangible as real (see, for example, Lather, 1993, 1995; Peters &
Burbules, 2004; St. Pierre & Pillow, 2000; Britzman, 2000;
Stronach & MacLure, 1997). It is a methodology that is constantly on the lookout for the specters, the mystics, and the
poets who wander just beyond the pale of the ordinary, the expected, or the possible. It is a methodology that will faithfully
signal to us that there are haunting discourses betraying the
thought and speech within the present boundaries, if only we
will pay attention. This methodology revels in being out of
joint, out of bounds, inhabited, excessive, and at times out of
control. It is a methodology that crosses borders, seeks sur-
prises, and produces excesses. It is a methodology and a reading of data that elevates the tension between the dominant
conventional analysis and the transgressive readings. (Caputo,

1997, p. 81). "It is exceedingly close, fine-grained, meticulous, scholarly, serious, and, above all, 'responsible,' both in the sense of being able to give an account of itself in scholarly terms and in the sense of 'responding' to something in the text that tends to drop out of view" (p. 77).

What could possibly be more irresponsible, more impossible, and more desirable? The "possible" limits that currently define research and confine data are transgressed and deconstructed in order to point us toward the impossible, the irresponsible, the unheard elements that invite our "text" to speak to us from beyond the limits of our received methodologies. A deconstructive methodology transgresses and in that trangression invites the excess, this impossible, and while I present strategies that I have engaged to employ this method in Chapters Six and Seven, it is forever important to remember that what I attempt is both impossible *and* irresponsible.

An Excessive Reading (or Listening)

In the context of qualitative research, and specifically in the case of my work with white teachers, I must continuously ask/clarify, what is this "text" that we consider in an analysis of the records of research? We are well advised to delineate artifacts or records that make up the "data" that count or that we consider as we attempt to make meaning of the words spoken by research participants. Relying in large part on the work of Derrida and others who use the signifier "text," it is important that I clarify that "text" does not refer to a "book," nor does it refer solely to that which is written, but rather inclusively to that which is communicated. Derrida further elaborates on the question of the text in stating, "If deconstruction really consisted in saying that everything happens in books, it wouldn't deserve five minutes of anybody's attention" (cited in Baker, 1995, p. 16).

Reflecting on Derrida's concept of the text, Bennington (cited in Royle, 2000) writes, "Text' is not quite an extension of a familiar concept, but a displacement or reinscription of it. Text in general is any system of marks, traces, referrals" (p. 7).

The text is not a limiting set of marks on a page, but is an opening up of words both written and spoken, of traces in speech and in writing. Writing is simply the paradigm while textuality is the sewing together of these traces. An excessive reading then serves to produce the pattern present in the text and highlights the stitching that holds that pattern together.

In the spirit of deconstruction and the excess I have been excessing over, the breach that opens itself to consideration is the breach into/out of the abyss. This abyss is, of course, not an abyss of nothingness, but of fullness; it is an absence, not as lack, but an absence as presence. It is an aporia, presented not for the purpose of being solved, but for the purpose of opening up the possibilities in an endless play of haunting. Thus if we are to expand the notion of "text" to that which is beyond the spoken, then we also must expand our notion of what "counts" as spoken. Silences and pauses must now be invited to step forward and take their rightful place in the pantheon of speech acts. These furtive wanderers can no longer masquerade as humble specters slipping in and out as unnamed, ignored disrupters. They can no longer frolic as traces, elusive and "meaningless." No, a deconstructive methodology will serve to expose them, to interrupt the sound barriers enabling their "meaning fullness" to be heard.

Derrida writes of deconstruction as a process of de-sedimentation (1976/1967, p. 10). Might then this deconstructive methodology involve a de-construction, a de-sedimentation of speech/text in order to give voice to the silent breath masked beneath the spoken words? Like so many beachcombers we dig and we sift, engaging in a process of de-sedimentation such that the silence beneath the spoken may be sorted and those masquerading specters be unveiled, found out. The excesses previously hidden become the pearls of great price, the excess that is no longer discarded or ignored, the impossible, a vital vocal part of the "total phenomena" (LeCompte & Preissle, 1993) present and attended to in our work as educational ethnographers.

An excessive reading further points to the need for strategies that enable us as researchers to sift these excesses and consider them alongside, within that which we have contained in our traditional understandings of text, speech, data. As

Cixous (1997/1994) describes the process, we engage in practices to recover "what is forgotten, subordinated" (p. 11). Part of the project of engaging in an excessive reading then is to consider these excesses in the text and the rhetorical practices potentially at work (e.g., purposeful deployment of silence on the part of the "speaker") in order that the silences may be reinscribed, not as voids or extraneous pauses, but as parts of the speech act, essential elements of the "play" of language. In other words (or without words), as readers/researchers we "must make room for 'the irruptive emergence of a new 'concept'" (Spivak, 1976, p. lxxvii), which embodies a spoken silence, a new impossible excess. My project is to recognize and make known that this excess is not marginal text, but rather, essential text. This excessive reading leads me "To locate the promising marginal text [i.e., silence], ...to pry it loose" and to dismantle the resident hierarchy "in order to reconstitute what is always already inscribed" (p. lxxvii).

Commensurate with this prying loose, Derrida depicts the task of deconstruction as intending to "'dismantle [deconstruire] the metaphysical and rhetorical structures which are at work in [the text], not in order to reject or discard them, but to reinscribe them in another way'" (quoted in Spivak, 1976, p. lxxv). A deconstructive method or reading then compels us to be unflinchingly open to the chance, the breach, the *impossible* possibility of silence. We are consigned to make room for the irruptive emergence of a new concept, a concept that no longer allows itself to be bound by the strictures of the previous regime where the spoken word is privileged as the only element that is discernible, intelligible, accessible, *meaning full*. What is contained in this excessive reading is the promise of a rupture that questions such privilege and revels in the impossible excess that transgresses in the beneath/beyond language of silence.

It should be noted that a deconstructive reading, an excessive reading of data will not provide yet another entrée for mastering the data, nor will it explain through a close reading of the text what the data or participants do not know, but rather, this reading will serve to point us to that which resides outside/within the significant chunk of the data that has previously been left out, ignored, not counted. Of course, that persistent question will be raised, "Why should we undo and redo a text at all? Why not assume that words and the author 'mean what they say?'" (Spivak 1976, p. lxxvii). Because in and through this process of sifting, we open the possibility of making visible that which was concealed in the layers of sediment (spoken words), those masked/discarded meanings which exist outside and beyond. An excessive reading does not "disregard" the spoken intent, rather it invites the impossible possible, the transgressive, irruptive moment which reveals (revels) in the pause, the breath, the silence—a speech act full of what the speaker didn't mean to mean to say and the researcher didn't mean to hear.

Silent Excesses

Jim Garrison (2004) writes that he begins "within texts signed 'Jacques Derrida' where I believe it fruitful for educators to begin" (p. 95). As Garrison and others have found, there are many fruitful openings and departure points through the writings of Derrida and those irruptions and breaches that deconstructive strategies prompt in terms of pedagogy, educational philosophy, and qualitative inquiry (Trifonas & Peters, 2004). Like Garrison, I am interested in an emphasis focused on how deconstruction, as a result of the work of Derrida, "opens questions about why certain practices become intelligible, valued, deemed as traditions, while other practices become impossible, denigrated or unimaginable" (p. 98). Using deconstruction as a strategy enables me to discern the haunting discourses that betray the spoken word. This approach has a unique quality in that through the use of deconstructive strategies I am also establishing a data set that is lacking in the methodological literature, namely silence. A deconstructive methodology legitimates the illegitimate possibility, or rather impossibility, of purposeful, meaningful data in the pauses, breaths, and avoidances present in the conversations with research participants. In short, this methodology freely cavorts with the elusive specters of silence welcoming them as actors in the play.

These pauses, breaths, avoidances, and other silences on the part of our participants are often marked in our transcripts by codes indicating a "gap" or diversion in the conversation with explanations such as she/he had nothing to say, or was thinking before responding, or went off on a tangent. These marked pauses are usually not considered as "parts of speech" or "text" or "data" to be counted, coded, and analyzed. We consider them initially as absences, voids, unintelligible gaps, or meaningless detours.[3]

Why are these silent specters so elusive, so hidden, and so often overlooked? Even when the silences present themselves to us, and we mark them on the page, we often fail to hear them. Why not let them speak? Is it because we have already "marked" them as irrelevant or unintelligible excesses, unimportant nuisances not to be dealt with? Derrida (1994/1993) provides another possible response in the following passage from *Specters of Marx*:

> Finally, the last one to whom a specter can appear, address itself, or pay attention is a spectator as such. At the theater or at school. The reasons for this are essential. As theoreticians or witnesses, spectators, observers, and intellectuals, scholars believe that looking is sufficient. Therefore, they are not always in the most competent position to do what is necessary: speak to the specter. Herein lies perhaps, among so many others, an indelible lesson of Marxism. There is no longer, there has never been a scholar capable of speaking of anything and everything while addressing himself to everyone and anyone, and especially to ghosts. There has never been a scholar who really, and as scholar, deals with ghosts. A traditional scholar does not believe in ghosts—nor in all that could be called the virtual space of spectrality. There has never been a scholar who, as such, does not believe in the sharp distinction between the real and the unreal, the actual and the inactual, the living and the non-living, being and non-being ("to be or not to be," in the conventional reading), in the opposition between what is present and what is not, for example in the form of objectivity. (p. 11)

How then to let the silences exist, breathe, or speak—*to be or not to be?* The problem is not our objectivity in the sense of seeing (or hearing) is believing, or even our thinking the possibility of silence, but rather embracing the ghost of silence as possibility (Derrida, 1994/1993, p. 12). The silent excesses that are legend in our texts are laden with the impossibility of existing, of speaking, of "the real," and they haunt the opening or crack through which we can hear their spectral voice. But in order to hear we must attend to the stoma that breathes the possibility of an irresponsible, impossible and more complete hearing, that teases us with a script, an elusive rendering beyond/outside our coded transcripts, an excess, if you will, a "playful" excess.

A *Play* of Silence

Play can be serious business. Borrowing once again from Derrida, I am not speaking of play as something trivial. My attempt to describe and employ a methodology that takes seriously those things that have been previously discounted *is* serious business. That is why I am serious about play! Might we then consider Derrida's playfulness and how a practice of maximizing the free play as a way to keep the structure of speech open within a play of silence might inform our practices of analysis and representation? This would, of course, also permit the play of absence in this pursuit of the play speech, not as absence, but as presence.

What then is play? One way that Derrida (1978/1968) describes play is as "the description of presence...Play is always play of absence and presence" (p. 292). But how does one consider this play of absence as presence in speech? As qualitative researchers, what do we put into play? How might I consider or talk about what I put into play in the analysis and representation that I seek? Derrida (1982/1972) further describes *différance* as a "playing movement that 'produces'" (p. 11). What then might be the playing movements of silence that if taken seriously, if considered plausible, or dare I say possible (impossible), would produce intelligible meaning? What might be produced by putting play into play in such a way as to discover *meaning full* silences—ones that are *play full*, or full of play?

Lest we not forget, and so we must listen to the whispers of the specters, play is a serious business and one that can produce previously unthought thoughts. This means that play is not only serious but dangerous. I wish to digress for a moment and look at how our traditional ways of using the word "play" might invite Derrida's form of "play" with the hope of a dangerous "play" of silence.

Play is (or can be) dramatic. A play enacts a tale involving the portrayal of people, relationships and stories. It functions through dialogue *and* breath; words *and* actions; speech *and* silence. Using this notion we treat our discourses as dramas in which thoughts, feelings, emotions and yes, silences, gasps, breaths, pauses, blanks, are used by participants to enact their tales. This attention to play as "enacting" brings those silences to center stage, gives them import and impels us to pay attention as we would to actors in those moments we call "pregnant pauses."

Play is also about being in the game, and one must be in the game in order to play. In order to play in the abyss of silence, as researchers we must first be playful—full of play. We must take seriously (without taking ourselves too seriously) the play of speech, the frolic of the specters that haunt the words and *play*-fully tease us to pay attention. Silence is the condition of irruption—that instant when we are open to laughter (in all seriousness) and free to hear outside our hearing.

Play is also a strategic move, a carefully designed action or coordinated series of actions with the goal of advancement, scoring, or defending a goal (*serious* play?). But in order to confuse the "opposition" one must use the element of surprise. (What could be more playful?) Strategy as play or play as strategy will destabilize our received notion of what "counts" in data collection so that the silences might break through the defense of our hearing and reveal something previously unthought. (Interesting that the opposition in this game is not just an "opponent" in a game-playing sense, but is our own reticence to romp with the specters. No wonder we need to play!)

It must be clear by now that if we are to *hear* silence, we must encourage silence to play and we must play in silence. Or, said another way, we must put silence into play. The sifting we as researchers employ in our analysis of "speech" and "text" will no longer permit a tossing out of those large chunks of silence that we at one time might have considered to be of little value if in fact we were to have noticed them at all. Using a deconstructive methodology, silence must now be allowed to play, to jump up and down, to bend the rules, remake the rules, toss out the rules. A play of silence (or playful silence) will take us back to the sandlot where play was less structured and more fun. We don't need an instant re-play because it doesn't matter if the play is out of bounds or the rules are ignored. No. Now we are ready to play, making it up as we go along, listening and re-listening to those meaning full absences, the silences that are laden with speech. What we know is that silence is firmly ensconced in the field of play, but this time the field or the pitch is more like that of Quidditch; it seems to have no boundaries at all.

Silence as *Différance*

This writing about the impossibility of a deconstructive methodology and of silence as *différance* created a power play between me and my computer's word processing program. It (the all knowing computer) became convinced that "it" was smarter than me in all things philosophical and kept changing *différance* to *difference*. This "knowing" computer replaced the intended word, signifier, idea, with its own trace. "It" failed to acknowledge that something else, something other, might be what was meant and attempted not to reinforce, but to erase my thought, my word, my trace, that "trace, which can be written but not spoken in the silent "a" of différance" (Taylor, 1986, p. 33). Well, outfoxing the "smart" machine, I reinserted the trace and reclaimed authorial authority, at least for that split second, for that space of an event. The "silent" computer, however, had taught me a lesson.

In his essay "Différance," Derrida (1982/1972) begins by speaking of a letter, of the letter *a* that is written but cannot be heard. And while he states one can "act as if it made no difference" (p. 3), it is significant in our understanding of the silent presence. He writes, "Thus, even if one seeks to pass over such an infraction in silence, the interest that one takes in it can be recognized and situated in advance as prescribed by the mute irony, the inaudible misplacement, of this literal permutation" (p. 3). It is the specter of this haunting, silent word play in which Derrida engages that summons me, demands a hearing, and breathes of "silent play," of "inaudible difference," of "inaudible misplacement," of "presence in absence." I am once again beckoned by the specter's siren.

Not just a letter, but a word, and the "silent play," or the "playing movement that 'produces'" (p. 11) emerges from a probing of this silent letter, this misspelled word, this voiceless trace. Scrutinizing the words again and again, the silent specter leaps from every page. "It cannot be apprehended in speech ...It is offered by a mute mark" (pp. 3-4). What is the promise of this silence? How does the specter of Derrida's *différance* answer?

> The same, precisely, is *différance* (with an *a*) as the displaced and equivocal passage of one different thing to another, from one term of an opposition to the other. Thus one could reconsider all the pairs of opposites on which philosophy is constructed and on which our discourse lives, not in order to see opposition erase itself but to see what indicates that each of the terms must appear as the *différance* of the other, as the other different and deferred in the economy of the same (the intelligible as differing-deferring the sensible, as the sensible different and deferred...) (p. 17).

A beckoning trace (siren) teases the possibility of spoken words and silent traces as the playful movement that brings forth, as the always already present, as the différance of the other. Such a response to a trace that can be written but not spoken is the field of play of silence as the différance that produces meaning—as meaning ignored and deferred. Is this perhaps the *secret*? That silence, masking as nothingness, as a specter, is in fact "as powerful as it is unreal, a hallucination or simulacrum that is virtually more actual than what is so blithely called a living presence" (Derrida, 1994/1993, p. 13).

Giving Up on the Secret

Lest I become overenthusiastic and think that I have solved the puzzle, cracked the code, outsmarted myself (and my computer), I am brought back to reality in the knowledge that there is no secret. There is no single answer, no undisputed truth, no silence decoder, no spoken pledge. There is no deconstructive methodology that reveals all the traces whether written or unwritten, silent or spoken, and then deems them intelligible. "If the readability of a legacy were given, natural, transparent, univocal, if it did not call for and at the same time defy interpretation, we would never have anything to inherit from it" (Derrida, 1994/1993, p. 16). If the answers were known, the play eliminated, the interpretation finalized, there would be no deconstruction, no search for a more complete meaning, for a better understanding. We could rely on the "evidence" of sight and sound as truth, as completeness, as gospel.

The certainty that there is no secret, no single meaning, no authoritative voice (either silent or spoken), should not lead us to despair. Rather, it impels us forward. It is when we respond to the siren call "of this secret, however, which points back to the other or to something else, when it is this itself which keeps our passion aroused, and holds us to the other, then the secret impassions us. Even if there is none, even if it does not exist, hidden behind anything whatever. Even if the secret is no secret, even if there has never been a secret, a single secret. Not one" (Derrida, 1992, p. 24).

Our texts, in the form of data generated from interviews with participants, are unmasterable, polyvocal, not containable, and because of this, we continue to search for the multiple meanings, voices, layers—not in hopes of learning the secret, but in hopes of remaining true to the passion of endless inquiry. "The passion of non-knowledge protects the future and keeps it open by keeping it secret—indeterminate, unforeseeable, unprogrammable—as opposed to confining it within the parameters of the possible" (Caputo, 1997, p. 103). The possibility of the secret is the condition of possibility, of what is not yet thought, not yet known, not yet possible. The possibility of the secret is the possibility of a deconstructive methodology. "But is this possible? Of course it is not; that is why it is the only possible invention of deconstruction...This impossible, unbelievable deconstruction would be the impossible, which pushes us beyond the tiresomeness of the possible" (Caputo, 1997, p. 115).

CHAPTER 3

An Absent Presence: Theorizing Silence

> Data analysis involves organizing what you have *seen, heard, and read* [emphasis mine] so that you can make sense of what you have learned.
>
> —Glesne, 1999, p. 130

Silence: A Fold in the Fabric

Qualitative researchers organize data and take careful note of what they see, what they hear and what they read, while lurking in the shadows, the specters haunt in the absent presence of the unseen, the unheard, the not read. Our participants are gracious to laden us with the pauses, the said but "not said," both intentional and unintentional silences. They give us the gift of their narratives and within that gift is the "other" gift that we do not always recognize, or miss through inattention, or negate as unimportant in favor of what we "perceive" as being more important. The gift within the gift is of course that pause—the not said, the reticent breath, the stark silence that transgresses our received notions of data and yet beckons us to identify it as something other than lack, or emptiness of meaning, or simply a distraction on the way to something "more important." Like an unwanted gift for which we feign appreciation but that we cast aside after the giver has taken leave, we leave this gift unclaimed and unappreciated. Yet, what if the unseen, the unheard, the not read is the essential gift or ground of the seen, the heard, and the read?

Merleau-Ponty (1964/1960) tells us that "Speech always comes into play against a background of speech; it is always only a fold in the immense fabric of language" (p. 42). The fold in the fabric of research that provides vitality, life and meaning to the seen, heard and read is the presence of silence through the unseen, unheard and not read. "Rather than being that which thwarts language, silence is that which opens the way for language's potency...speech is born from silence and seeks its conclusion in silence....Silence, then, is required for the intelligibility both of what is said in discourse and of discourse itself as discourse" (Dauenhauer, 1980, p. 119). The implications of the potency to be found in the fold of qualitative data, and particularly discourse-based data, are considerable. And yet, this examination of silence as critical to language is, as one might expect, also elusive. What is "seen, heard, and read," must be reconceptualized in order to "listen" for the potency of the silent discourses.

One aspect of my work is situated in the context of white teachers engaged in conversations of race, culture, and difference. Drawing on the parallels of whiteness theory, my work seeks a development of silence theory, or rather a theorizing of silence. Theorizing silence is much like theorizing whiteness. The absences are present, yet elusive; they are demanding, yet invisible, much like the specters present in Derrida's deconstruction. It is a continued fascination with these specters of silence and their haunting responses that gives impetus to my research.

A conceptualization and theorizing of silence is always mindful of Dyer (1988) writing of whiteness as often feeling as if there is no subject at all. "The colourless multi-colourdness of whiteness secures white power by making it hard, especially for white people and their media to 'see' whiteness. This, of course, makes it very hard to analyze...The subject seems to fall apart in your hands before you begin" (p. 46).

My theorizing of silence seeks to make present that voice which is absent, to posit the silences of our research participants as purposeful rhetorical strategies. Derrida (1992) maintains that silence is indeed a strategic response (p. 18). The approach I pursue seeks to lend credibility and therefore cause for a vital examination of those strategic responses that we might previously have overlooked or ignored as unimportant. Listening to these silences and attending to the strategic moves will tell us much about those who inhabit our field sites and the context in which they live. Merleau-Ponty asserts that "we should be sensitive to the thread of silence from which the tissue of speech is woven" (cited in Dauenhaueer, 1980, p. 116). Our attention to these threads of silence that might, so easily, fade into the background of the fabric of speech will now be recognized as a vital part of the whole, and without which would leave a tapestry only incompletely embracing its subject, a tapestry laden with gaps and missed stitches.[1]

Through a recognition and probing of these silences, the pulling on these threads so cleverly woven, the hearing of these haunting specters, we might begin to sense a form of the subject who does seem to "fall apart in your hands before you begin." This theorizing of silence locates silence as "data," not as absence, lack, or omission, but as positive, strategic, purposeful, and *meaning full.* Using the literature of communication theory, linguistics, psychotherapy, literary theory, poetry, and philosophy I will approach means of exploring these silent ghosts as worthy of our hearing.

Locating Silence

Silences are ubiquitous in the conversations between/with qualitative researchers and their participants. While the disciplines of psychotherapy (see, e.g., Strean, 1990; Cook, 1964) and communication theory (see, e.g., Saville-Troike, 1985; Tannen & Saville-Troike 1985; Tannen 1989; Jaworski, 1993, 1997) explore silence as purposeful, a discussion of silence in discourse-based methodological literature and the social sciences often refers only to the silencing of stories (see, e.g., Lather, 1996; Lewis & Simon, 1986) or explores the power of normative discourses that produce silence (see Russel y Rodríguez, 1998; Jackson, 2006). My focus is not one of a methodology that engages the silencing of stories, nor am I primarily concerned with how the power of normative discourses produce silence. Rather, my use of a deconstructive methodology is for the purpose of a theorizing of silence as data, as a type of transgressive data (St. Pierre, 1997), that when taken seriously, is allowed to enter the playing field of discourse-based research. And because silence has not been treated as data, or even as positive expression in qualitative inquiry, the focus of a methodology that posits silence as data seeks to establish silence as an integral component of our gathered discourse to be attended to with the same "ear" as that which is accorded the privileged distinction of having been "spoken."

The tradition of silence as being, as presence, as spoken, is long in the context of philosophy, art, literature, poetry and music. An elucidating example of this is provided in the opening paragraphs of her book, *The Language of Silence*, as Ernestine Schlant (1999) vividly describes such rendering that occurs when sculpture speaks through an absence.

> In Berlin, outside the Grunewald train station where the trains left for Auschwitz, there is a monument to those who were deported and killed. It is a long straight wall of exposed concrete, perhaps 15 feet high, which appears to hold back the earth rising up behind it. Cut into the wall are the outline of human figures moving in the direction of the station. The figures themselves are nonexistent; it is the surrounding cement that makes their absence visible. (p. 1)

My theorizing of silence is an attempt to demonstrate how silence speaks through the concrete of the spoken in our transcripts and conversations. I do this in search of a silent discourse whose haunting of the "text" has many stories to tell and secrets to unravel.

A Search for the Whole

In 1955–56, Martin Heidegger gave a lecture course at the University of Freiburg, published as *The Principle of Reason*. One of Heidegger's methodological moves is a probing of that which is self-evident, toward that which is not self-evident or superficial, to that which he terms as being what really matters. He expounds upon Leibnitz's "Principle of Ground" and explores why something that is to us now so self-evident, that is the premise that *nothing* is without reason, took us centuries to recognize.

Methodologists attempting to destabilize received methodologies and understandings talk about the process of "making the familiar strange" in order that we pay close attention in data analysis to those things previously overlooked because they are so commonplace. This seems an accurate description of an attempt to recognize that which is seemingly self-evident and hence overlooked as familiar—the unnoticed, the unheard, embodied in a deconstructive analysis of silence as part of the whole in discourse-based research. A process that strives to make the familiar strange seeks to resist a tendency to "elide" silence as that which is common or "understandable" without introducing the quality of "strangeness" which results in a stoppage, an exploration of this absent presence.

This is not unlike the strangeness we encounter in struggling with a different language. "When we hear a foreign language which we speak poorly; we find it monotonous and marked with an excessively heavy accent and flavor, precisely because we have not made it the principal instrument of our relations with the world" (Merleau-Ponty, 1964/1960, p. 55). In qualitative research, silence is or can be this "foreign" language to which we do not attend as it has not been the "principal instrument" of our interaction with the world, thus we find it uncomfortable or unfathomable or seemingly unimportant because, like a foreign language, we cannot readily glean meaning and a depth of understanding. And so we ignore this "speech," bide our time, until the conversation returns to "our" language. A theorizing of silence proposes that we proceed by making the familiar strange, but in so doing we must also recognize that the "familiarity" of silence is already strange to us, unfamiliar to us, and thus requires an even more nuanced attentiveness. When we recognize silence as this familiar occurrence but also as an unfamiliar "foreign" language in the midst of spoken data we will adjust our listening to a more intentional and nuanced ear that is ready to hear silence as a complex phenomenon.

Bernard Dauenhauer (1980) in the book *Silence: The Phenomenon and Its Ontological Significance* presents an ontological interpretation of silence, and an assertion of silence as a positive and complex phenomenon. Building on the work of Merleau-Ponty, he writes of silence as an active performance and therefore an integral aspect of communication. Further, he writes of silence as the ground of speech, in other words, returning to Heidegger's assertion that "nothing is without reason" [or ground], silence is the ground without which speech cannot happen. A search for the whole of speech is not possible without a commensurate search for the silence therein.

This search for the whole and an awareness of silence is epitomized by one of my earlier research projects. The "reams" of collected data included hours of transcripts and notes in my conversations with white teachers examining race (specifically their/our own) and how an understanding of themselves as raced might impact their interactions with students, particularly as it influenced decisions regarding curricular choices, pedagogy, and classroom management. However, absent from the growing stack of data, or at least my perceived notion of the data, were the silences, the "positive" productive silences. Of course, although it was not clear at the time, the silent discourses seemed unfathomable because my analysis was concerned only with attending to the perceived presence of fullness in articulated speech rather than a wholistic attention to absence in presence-filled silence.

While drowning in this "sea" of data I had begun a parallel venture of immersing myself in the world of poetry as a way to develop my writing and to cultivate a less restrictive means of an analysis and representation of my research. The biannual Dodge Poetry Festival served as one important event in this undertaking. During the Festival a session entitled "Spoken Poems and Silent Readings" caught my attention. The session involved several poets discussing the silences in poetry and how these purposeful pauses were not experienced as absences or mere breaths, but as essential to the meaning and rhythm of the poems. Listening to their talk of silence was as if someone had dumped an entirely new set of transcripts in my lap. It was then that what had until that time been considered the "thinness" of my data was diverted by a growing sense of the possibility of "thick description" (Geertz, 1973) that might be discovered through a more informed scrutiny.

The "text" of my data was indeed voluminous, but even so, many topics germane to the discourse were in fact absent from what had been seen, heard, and recorded. Following the session with the poets it seemed obvious (finally) that the "thin-ness" of the data simply reflected the reality that a substantial portion of it had been disregarded, not allowed to "speak" through its silence. It was not that the silence was absent, but that I was deaf to its subtle voice. Of course, now that silence had the sliver of an opening it began to haunt me and expose itself as a ubiquitous presence both inside and outside the text. This released an unrelenting obsession on my part to not only attend to silence as speech but to hear it everywhere and to wonder why we were not, as researchers, more attuned to its presence. It seemed clear now that there was a need to address the methodological implications of silence as necessary for in-telligibility in a search for the whole. If as qualitative research-ers we are to adhere to the assertion that "Silence, then, is required for the intelligibility both of what is said in discourse and of discourse itself as discourse" (Dauenhauer, 1980, p. 119), then it is imperative to acknowledge a substantial data set to which we have previously failed to attend.

In the article "The Pressure to Cover," legal scholar Kenji Yoshino (2006) writes about the process of playing down one's outsider identities in order to fit into the mainstream as the act of "covering." In describing his initial encounter with this phe-nomenon he wrote, "As is often the case when you learn a new idea, I began to perceive covering everywhere...spotting in-stances of covering felt like a parlor game" (p. 34). My experi-ence with silence as data has been very similar. Since beginning this project, I have accumulated a file drawer of arti-cles in the popular media about silence in politics, art, and theater. Some examples of these popular culture references in-clude: what was left out of film adaptations of historical events and why, stories or accusations that politicians failed to com-ment on, communities being shrouded in silence after a local disaster, and the use of silence in films to create characters of strength and intentionality. Books outside the fields of educa-tion and qualitative research that I might not have previously considered have landed on my shelf because they contain the word "silence" in the title, for instance: *The World of Silence* by Picard (1988), *Organizing Silence* by Clair (1988), and *On Lies, Secrets, and Silence* by Rich (1979) to name just a few. And when I have described my project to both academics and non-academics, there is a response that signals, "of course, silence can be intentional." However, a treatment or hearing of silence does not just happen. As we find described by Dauenhauer (1980) in a discussion of Kierkegaard: One "cannot not just launch into the topic," nor listen passively, nor attempt an incomplete analysis. One must first "attune himself [sic] to hear that which he seeks to understand" and listen with effort (p. 112).

Between Words

> But what if language expresses as much by what is between words as by the words themselves? By that which it does not 'say' as by what it 'says.' (Merleau-Ponty, 1964/1960, p. 45)

As literate beings, and particularly as academics, our attention, our focus, our work, is centered on words, words that we speak, words that we hear, words that we write, words that we read—words, words, words. This myopia regarding "expressed sound" would seem to fall under a severe critique if we take seriously Merleau-Ponty's assertion that language is as expressive *between* words as *with* words. We must reconsider just how much of the meaning of our discourse is being missed when we do not apprehend the "between words" discourse. This search for the *meaning full* insists that we be constantly aware that "Speech points beyond itself to the silence, to the word within the word, the language buried in language" (Brown cited in Clair, 1998, p. 23).

To attend to the words between words, or the language buried in language, is to conceive of the silences as intelligible elements of language. These silent "words" are intelligible and forceful in the image evoked by Schlant. It is their absence that makes them visible, but it is this very absence that requires a different listening, a listening for the words between words. In the same way that Schlant describes the figures as only present because of the absence, Picard (1988) writes that speech cannot exist without silence. "The word would be without depth if the background of silence were missing" (p. 28), in the same way that the sculpture would be without depth, without the same impact, without the presence of absence.

This depth of which Picard speaks can be likened to the meaning embedded in the depths of silence as described by Dauenhauer (1980), "the silence of the to-be-said...the silence of the what-ought-to-be-said in which what-is-said is embedded" (p. 19). Given this understanding, the silences are pregnant with what is to be said but cannot be said, just yet, of the ought-to-be-said, but that which is unutterable due to the possible repercussions, and the what-is-said, the meanings conveyed more loudly in silent speech.

The words between words, the silent words, are also not absences, are not "a passive background to the noisy activity of communication" (Clair, 1998, p. 8), but contained within them are meanings purposeful and unintentional, intelligible and unintelligible, apparent and sedimented. These words between words are not merely an absence of something else; they are an integral aspect of the fullness of expression. This is particularly evident in our experience that participants are not always silent because they cannot find the right words or have nothing to say. Sometimes the words between words are spoken because participants have everything to say and words are not sufficient, words cannot say enough—or hide enough.

Li Li (2004) describes how a goal of education often involves a filling of the gaps of silence in order to avoid an interruption of "the process of knowledge transmission" (p. 71). What is missed by educators given this negative orientation toward silence is that in silence, "there is something of the spoken word" (Picard, 1988, p. 24). Silence is speech, and if our attempts focus on filling these silent gaps, then we preclude the possibility of the meanings lost in the silences, in the words between words.

Poetic Silences

Addressing an audience at the 1996 Dodge Poetry Festival in the session Spoken Poems and Silent Readings, Briget Pegeen Kelly (1996) spoke of silence as "inhabited"—inhabited signifying meaning and breath in the silences. Gerald Stern (1996) further elaborated that there is an awareness of the presence of silence in the uttering of poetry. Robert Hass (1996) stated that poets look for ways to tap into feelings and emotions in the silences, describing those silences as the breath and the life of living. Many poets further this idea by speaking of the life of their poems as being found in the breath, the pauses, or the unwritten cadences.[2]

In a poem entitled "Enough Words?" Rumi, a thirteenth-century mystic and poet speaks of the soul as living in the "silent breath" (Rumi, 1995, p. 20–21). Coleman Barks in his discussion of Persian poetry indicated that Rumi, instead of referring to himself at the end of his poems, a customary practice for the time, ended over a thousand poems with reference to Shams or silence. "He gives the poetry to its true authorship, including the emptiness after as part of the poem...Words are not important in themselves, but as resonators for a center" (in Rumi, 1995, p. 17). In the closing stanzas of the poem "Only Breath," Rumi (p. 32) illuminates this place of talk in silence and breath:

> There is a way between voice and presence
> where information flows.
>
> In disciplined silence it opens.
> With wandering talk it closes.

What Rumi illustrates in "Only Breath" is the possibility of meaning that occurs in disciplined or purposeful silences. The purposeful silences permit meaning, while the wandering talk of meaningless words do not. The disciplined silences create an opening for the potency of silent language.

While Kelly, Stern, Hass, and Barks speak of the metaphorical silences in poetry, Langston Hughes (1994, p. 234) has written a poem in which he illustrates the literal silences present, or rather absent, in our speech, and how they are laden with meaning.

Silence

I catch the pattern
Of your silence
Before you speak.

I do not need
To hear a word.

In your silence
Every tone I seek
Is heard.

The tones to which Langston Hughes refers can be linked to the strategic silences of Derrida and of the words between words of Merleau-Ponty. Hughes presents a poetic description of the patterns and meaning communicated perhaps more forcefully, more "disciplined," more purposefully, than if they were voiced. These silent tones also gesture toward that which links voiced words and silent words as complementary of one another. Although "the nature of communication structured through talk is different from the nature of communication structured through silence," as asserted by Jaworski (1993, p. 47), he additionally states that "silence and speech complement each other in the linguistic universe and they are capable of performing similar functions and expressing similar meanings" (p. 47).

A furthering of a poetic understanding of silence can be found in the writing of literary theorists. While discussing the role of silence in literature, Schlant (1999) states, "Literature lays bare a people's dreams and nightmares, its hopes and apprehensions, its moral positions and its failures. It reveals even where it is silent; its blind spots and absences speak a language stripped of conscious agendas" (p. 3). In an analysis of silence in the works of Spanish novelist Carmen Martín Gaite, García (2000) affirms a privileged position for silence in prose when she states "silences in narrative can be as articulate and ambiguous as words" (p. 10). For example, García discusses how in literature written during the Franco era, silences were present due to the threat of official censorship and in doing so she also presents examples of marked audible silences in the fiction of this time (p. 47).

Additionally, Terry Eagleton (1983) speaks of the "subtexts" and "blindness" present in literary works as revealing assumptions that are not articulated, and possibly not known, but present nonetheless. "The work's insights, as with all writing, are deeply related to its blindnesses: what it does not say, and *how* [emphasis in original] it does not say it, may be as important as what it articulates; what seems absent, marginal or ambivalent about it may provide a central clue to its meanings" (p. 178).

Through these ideas and assertions we more fully acknowledge the importance of silence as an essential element in embracing the "whole" of speech and its critical significance in the field of discourse-based research. As I will continue to argue, prerequisite in an understanding of the words between words as important in our continuing work as researchers is an acknowledgment of the unspoken or absent presence of these "words" as *meaning full* in our examination of discourse and the silences that give these discourses both form and substance.

Speaking the Unspeakable

> A woman remained silent. Long after the imposed silence associated with the mourning period was lifted, a widow from the Warramunga society chose to remain silent. Although the 'mourning silence' is imposed on the women for a period of two years, this woman remained silent for twenty-four years. Her silence speaks to us. It speaks of oppression; it enunciates defiance; it articulates resistance. Furthermore, it evidences creativity; it demonstrates control; it languishes in frustration; and it isolates the woman while simultaneously joining her to others who have known or know of the imposed silence. Her silence speaks at the local level to the Warramunga community; the stories of her silence speak to generations of Warramunga people and beyond to you and me. It is both a local story and the collective story of all women. (Clair, 1998, p. 147)

Speaking without speaking is not a new phenomenon. The ancient Hebrews recognized this in the silent speaking of Yahweh in the scriptures. Poets and musicians purposefully incorporate silences and breaths in their art when they include pauses in the spacing and performance of their expressions. Spouses and partners are silent when they are afraid of creating a chasm that cannot be repaired. Children refrain from answering questions in school when they know the answer, but withhold for fear of being labeled a "know-it-all," a "teacher's pet," or, if the answer is wrong, a "dummy." So why is it that in the context of qualitative inquiry, we have been so long in recognizing how the stories that our participants have to share are present in their speaking without speaking?

In writing of West German literature and the Holocaust, Schlant (1999) attends not to the "silences *of* the Holocaust" as she refers to them, silences performed because of the horror of the atrocities committed, but the "silences *about* the Holocaust," and in the context of her work, an absence of talk about the Holocaust in the East German non-Jewish literature for nearly 40 years following the war. She describes the literature of this period as a literature of "silence contoured by language" (p. 1). She further describes the way in which this period of literature speaks between words. "Silence is not a semantic void; like any language, it is infused with narrative strategies that carry ideologies and reveal unstated assumptions. Silence is constituted by the absence of words but is therefore and simultaneously the presence of their absence" (p. 7).

What are the silences *about* whiteness, racism, homophobia, or sexism, for example, that are not spoken *with* words, but are spoken *between* words? This speech between words is prevalent in research that probes these uncomfortable spaces because often for the participants their thoughts are unspeakable.[3] What is necessary is a recognition of these silences not just as semantic voids, but as unstated assumptions. What do research participants consider unspeakable because of what they may reveal about themselves, their prejudices, their ignorances, or their tolerances that they perceive as being unacceptable to others? Rather than assume that these unarticulated words are secondary to those spoken, should we not probe them for the unspeakable, the unspoken, the silent threads woven into our participant's tapestry of speech?

Jaworksi (1993) affirms that a simplistic view of silence treats silence as a lack of communication, but that if one is to examine a body of work on nonverbal communication, one is to find that "the absence of speech does not imply the absence of communication, and very frequently the interpretation of speech itself relies very heavily on the nonverbal component of communication" (p. 46). In other words, speaking without speaking is understood as a view of silence that places it not in opposition to speech, but that positions silent speech on a continuum with voiced speech.

This purposeful consideration of the unspoken or the unspeakable presents a more wholistic understanding of the narrative stories collected as data. Again, describing the silence of German literature, Schlant (1999) cautions that the silences themselves are not uniform or monolithic. The silences are deployed through a vast array of narrative strategies that have "delineated and broken these contours, in a contradictory endeavor to keep silent about the silence and simultaneously make it resonate." (p. 1). The silences then are not to be considered as "one" any more than we are to consider the spoken word as the "complete story." Thus, a theorizing of silence that is meaningful in the context of qualitative inquiry must be one that is nuanced, strategically deployed differently at different times, and that both keeps the silence and breaks the silence simultaneously.

Keeping Silent

In his contribution to the collection of essays entitled *Legacies and Ambiguities: Postwar Fiction and Culture in West Germany and Japan*, Peter Schneider (1991) recounted the following:

> I had the feeling of growing up in a permanent shadow, in some gray, unclear substance that covered memories and feelings, as if I could look at reality only through a tinted glass. Nobody would speak out. I remember those silent lunches, where I heard only the clinking of knives and forks. The absence of speech and laughter were more disturbing to me than anything I might have heard about World War II. (p. 281)

The silence on the part of older family members who had lived through the atrocities of WWII in Germany were positive expressions of words not spoken. Because what had happened was "unspeakable," it was not spoken, but in not speaking, the silent words fell heavier on the ear than if voiced.

Keeping silent, being silent, or not speaking, are all examples of what we might consider discursive moves. They are not to be understood as negative, in other words, not as absence or lack. They are, for Heidegger, examples of the nothing, the nothing as something we experience or encounter in language (Caputo, 1978, p. 19). Heidegger considered a search for the "nothing" as a search for the whole—without the nothing the whole is not possible. The whole that we seek in the records of research is congruent with an understanding of the "transparent" silences and the "obscuring" words as described by Heidegger in *Being and Time*. This silence is not an end in itself, as in negative theology, but a "caesura" within language, not beyond language but a linguistic operation residing therein.[4]

> *Keeping silent* [emphasis in original] is an essential possibility of discourse. In talking with one another, the person who keeps silent can 'make one understand' (that is, he can develop an understanding), and he can do so more authentically than the person who is never short of words. Speaking at length [Viel-sprechen] about something does not offer the slightest guarantee that thereby understanding is advanced. On the contrary, talking extensively about something, covers it up and brings what is understood to a sham clarity—the unintelligibility of the trivial. (Heidegger, 1962/1927, p. 208)

As qualitative researchers, this means that we are wise to re-consider the possibility of the presence of missed meanings that are conveyed by our participants in "idle talk." We are encouraged to probe the "words" (and the absence of words) that are carefully chosen by those with whom we converse in our research endeavors to "cover up" in favor of the unintelligibility of the trivial. This possibility of our participants purposefully "keeping silent" leads us to posit this reticence not just as an essential possibility of discourse but as an essential condition of discourse and further validates the movement toward a more complete, more nuanced understanding of our data.

We must attempt, then, to parse the "gain" of this practice of "keeping silent" and its effects for our participants. We need to be cognizant of the oppressions, the defiance, the ignorance, and the bigotries that are contained in and that exceed the silences in the to-be-said or ought-to-be-said as described by Dauenhauer (1980). When considering such content in an analysis of discourse-based research, an awareness of how the meanings are masked in the spoken and likewise present in the silent are imperative in a search for the whole. This methodological engagement with the silences again finds Heidegger (1962b/1927) helpful in an analysis of what he terms "idle-talk," talk that fills silence, but presents only the possibility of superficial understandings. "What is said-in-the-talk gets understood; but what the talk is about is understood only approximately and superficially" (p. 212), because the tendency is to focus on the obvious, on what is "seen, heard, or read," (Glesne, 1999) unless of course one begins to open up the possibility (or impossibility) of listening to/for the silences that, although cloaked initially, when unveiled serve to present a more meaningful and nuanced understanding.

Our role as researchers is to undress this cloaked silence, to engage everything it has to say, to pay attention not just long enough to conclude that what it has to say is simple and self-evident, but as a portraitist, to look closely with a keen eye so that we see the interior, the layers of paint and glazing that give meaning and life to the painting, to the text. In discussing Heidegger's critique of metaphysics, Caputo (1986) tells us that "Heidegger wants to hear what is drowned out for the rest of us" (p. 67). That then is the project not of *keeping silent*, but of *keeping the silences* as data that we consider in the records of research. Furthermore, a deconstructive methodology, a playful examination or reexamination of the "text," moves us to pay attention to the discourse in a different way, to listen to the silences, spoken or unspoken with renewed interest. Returning to Dauenhauer (1980), an attentiveness to the practice of keeping silent on the part of our research participants might lead to a better understanding of the to-be-said and the ought-to-be-said, embedded in what-is-said dialogue (p. 18).

Out of the silence, the specter issues a caveat, but only if we are paying close attention. It is false to claim that everything we glean through conversations and observations is a sham, or is trivial. It is also important to realize that not every silence or incidence of idle speech is laden with significance. But our grounding as qualitative researchers tells us that we mustn't accept what we are told on face value, that we need to spend extended time in the field and with our notes, and we also need to speak to participants in their variety of experiences and perspectives. That said, we can heed the caveat and still enter the field of play with all its attending possibilities and exhilarations, with just a little fear and trembling and a lot of frivolity. Keeping the silences means that we, like Hamlet and Derrida, seek out the specters that haunt the discourses. Keeping the silences means that we seek out the wisdom of these specters in search of the unguarded silences, those that have much to teach us, should we be courageous (and playful) enough to let them enter the gate.[5]

CHAPTER 4
A Problematic of Silence

> We want to try...to practise...[an] infidelity to educational research, in the hope of opening up connections and questions that are hard to see from within the space that marks its usual territories.
> —Stronach & MacLure, 1997, p. 4

Toward a Problematic of Silence

As I move toward a problematic of silence, I am more fully cognizant of the spaces and voices that mark the accepted territory for me as a qualitative researcher and how this territory delimits spoken words as the sole text from which meaning is made. Stronach and MacLure (1997) embrace deconstruction in educational research as an opening, a rupture, resistant to containment. A problematic of silence attempts to rupture that which inscribes the meanings and sources of meanings possible in the doing of qualitative research. In keeping with Heidegger's thinking at the limits of philosophy, a problematic of silence seeks to engage the limits of research that restrain our ability to hear the silences spoken by our participants.

This methodological incision is naturally unfaithful to any territorial dictates and irrupts with strategies that reveal connections or that permit a listening that has not been possible, that has literally been *impossible*, from the traditional demarcations of data, speech, meaning, etc. Toward this end, such a move takes seriously a dialogue with St. Pierre's (1997) positing of transgressive data sources to include silent data within this redefined/undefined space. Such a methodological move is possible not only through an exploration of the current problematic, but through a realignment of the problematic and a reappropriation of the terminology and the discourse. Lakoff and Johnson (1980) write about our conceptual systems as being ordered by metaphors that shape our perception of reality, an ordering of which we are often unaware. In the context of educational and social research, MacClure (2003) further extends the discussion not only of the metaphors that structure our discursive realities, but also of the binary structures that do the same.

Therefore, I use the notion of a problematic not simply to outline a new delimiting territory, but to strategically include what has been left out, excluded, and literally silenced. To engage a problematic of silence in qualitative inquiry is to begin a process of listening to our selves listening in an effort to recognize/identify what has been heard and what has been missed or ignored. A problematic of silence engages the idea presented in Chapter Two, prompted by my reading of Royle (2000), encouraging an openness to that which cannot be thought in the current context. A caution of course is that I do not fall prey to this problematic as simply another delimiting force.

In writing of conceptual structures termed problematics, Giroux (1988) explained, "problematics refer not only to what is included in a worldview, but also, to what is left out and silenced. That which is not said is as important as that which is said" (p. 4). It is this premise that leads to the important realization that in the doing of qualitative research, specifically discourse-based research, the absence in an analysis of conversations with research participants has often been the inclusion of silence. This lack is not because the silences have not been present, but because they have either not been recognized, or they have been "silenced." It is a poststructuralist understanding, particularly a deconstructive reading, that provides a theoretical framework to not only recognize these silences as purposeful and meaningful in consideration of the data, but to welcome their *meaning full speech* in our engagement with the text. Further, to explicate and demonstrate the ways in which a poststructural analysis shifts the problematic not only for the doing of qualitative research, but for encountering in a different way the results of that research.

Having presented deconstruction as a methodological strategy for considering silence, and having theorized silence using literary and philosophical discussions, my next move is toward the presentation of a problematic of silence that exposes the current boundaries of research and that re-imagines those boundaries in an attempt to expand the circumference of what is knowable, askable, and possible. A problematic of silence will prompt us as researchers to re-think how we consider data—what counts as data, what gets left out, and what gets left in. Such a problematic has the potential of irrupting our tightly demarcated understandings of discourse-based data as only being that which can be read in the printed words of a transcript. In other words, to return to Derrida, it breaks open the notion of "text" and what counts as "text." Or as MacClure writes (2003), it is a call for "learning, or choosing, to 'read' educational events and situations as *texts.*"

Just as Scheurich (1997) troubles the idea of when an interview begins and ends, this interruption of data troubles the idea of when data begins and ends; i.e., because a participant doesn't speak, chooses not to speak, or stops speaking, does this constitute the "end" of data? A problematic of silence presents considerations for how to think about discourse-based research, and if what counts as data includes silence, how this shapes or changes both the structure of the interview, the process of follow-up, and ultimately analysis and representation of data. The gaps and pauses are to be considered not as the boundaries of speech, but rather as an irruption of speech, an irruption that is essential to a fuller meaning of speech.

In my research with white teachers working in multiracial schools, we probed the notion of ourselves as whites having a racial identity. Following each session the tapes of the group conversation were transcribed in preparation for our next meeting. I listened for unanswered questions: sentences, phrases, expressions not finished; or topics that elicited awkward or strained interaction. At the conclusion of our first series of meetings, I reviewed all the transcripts in order to acquire a more complete analysis of both the scope and nuance of the conversations. This rereading soon resulted in an inchoate frustration at what was not being discussed not to mention a growing discomfort that the discussions had resulted in "thin data." My initial presumption was that this absence of substance in the conversations around certain topics or the evidence of questions not being answered was a result of the participants having nothing to say. Saville-Troike (1985) suggests, "Perhaps because silence in communicative settings is often taken simply for inaction,...the important position of silence...has been largely overlooked" (p. 15). As she so aptly points out, I was overlooking the important position of silence and wrongly interpreting it as inaction, disinterest, or nonresponse.

Not only was I overlooking the important position of silence, I was failing to consider silence as "text." A problematic of silence presupposes the important position of silence as a productive and purposeful element of the speech act. Further, it distinguishes between silence that serves the role of structuring communication and is thus an absence of sound, and that silence which is part of communication in the form of a speech act. A problematic of silence within the context of qualitative research considers silence as an element of communication on the part of both research participants and researchers. While Maxine Greene describes absence as suggesting an emptiness or, "a void to be filled, a wound to be healed, a flaw to be repaired" (1993, p. 14), I wish to understand silence as inhabited and therefore legitimated in what counts as empirical material to be considered. Silence is not merely a void hungering for noise, or a flaw to be mended, but is an essential part of the whole of language, the meaningful and purposeful "unobtrusive trace" of naturalistic inquiry (Lincoln & Guba, 1985) that beckons us to entertain its voice.

Listening to the Voices of Silence

Frederick Buechner (1977), novelist and theologian, discusses the deafening nature of silence, deafening because of the truths revealed in the silences should we give them a hearing.

> The preacher is not brave enough to be literally silent for long, ...even if he were brave enough, he would not be silent for long because we are none of us very good at silence. *It says too much* [emphasis mine]. (p. 23)

Silence does make us uncomfortable, and, if given a serious hearing, does say too much. Patti Lather (1996) writes of being invested as an author in "a practice that erases itself at the same time as it produces itself. Such a practice makes space for returns, silence, interruptions...Such a practice ignites in writing and reading [and listening] what is beyond the word and the rationally accessible" (pp. 531-532). It is important, then, not to fall into the trap of supplanting the silence with one's own voice, fears, desires, or omissions, but rather to "make space" for the returns, the interruptions, the resistances, the denials, the subtle eliding of text present in the unspoken.

As researchers it is essential that we forge this space for the silence to breathe and inform as we listen to the tapes of our conversations and read transcripts and journal reflections. This way of listening will encourage us to invite the voices present in the silences, rather than avoiding them. It will allow us to hear that which is being erased (silent breath) in the production of speech. It will encourage us to permit the expansion of spaces for the silence to fill, rather than filling the spaces of silence with meaningless noise, or with echoes of our own insecurities. Alison Jones (1999) describes this as a process of "breaking down 'the culture of silence'" in an effort to give voice to that which is produced beneath the layers of a hegemonic discourse. It was in this space, the space where the culture of silence was engaged, that the silences present in my conversations with the aforementioned white teachers began to reveal our level of participation in this hegemonic discourse. Through the strategic deployment of silence, white privilege continued to remain unspoken and therefore perpetuated. Racist assumptions and statements were made and not challenged, thereby reproducing this hegemony.

Russel y Rodríguez (1998) observes what she names as "anthropology's silencing praxis." She discusses how anthropology as a discipline silences due to its history, theoretical nature, and methods that demand static and untroubled identities of its subjects and practitioners—in other words, a reinscription of a hegemonic discourse. It is this demand for locating and fixing subjectivities that leads to silencing of both normative and oppositional stances. Congruent with Jones' assertion, it is necessary to recognize how the hegemonic or normative discourse serves to silence and reframe those oppositional stances so that they are silently articulated for fear of repercussions. Because they are "silently" articulated they are heard as a tacit acceptance of the silencing praxis that she describes.

In one of the group discussions with this group of white teachers, Marcy recounts the following incident.

> When I worked at Rosewood for a year, I really didn't have a lot of experience working with an all-black classroom, so the personnel director said I'm going to give you a class on the black race 101.
>
> 1. Your classroom is going to be noisy.
> 2. They don't sit still.
> 3. They're verbal learners, they're not auditory.
> 4. They hear by talking, don't give them a worksheet, they won't even read it, they don't read, they're just verbal, they talk.
>
> She said, it will be a lot different than anything you have ever done. And she was right. She said anything that you think might be a good idea, it might not work. This idea where I do a coordinated wardrobe from a J Crew catalog, that was a disaster, these were all girls, it was a summer program, and it was hard finding things that worked. Nothing worked for a long time, but finally it worked.
>
> But she was right. I just didn't think I was teaching if I didn't write it down and they didn't read it. I didn't think that that was learning.

Following this "lesson," the comments by the other teachers amounted to a silent acceptance of these fixed subjectivities and a reinscription of the hegemonic discourse. Not everyone agreed with this so-called approach to teaching, but faced with such a blanket and essentializing narrative, why was the response a resounding silence? I attempted to shift the conversation to an examination of how we make assumptions about our Other students and the resulting problems that may occur because of these assumptions. While Marcia did not condone what Marcy had said, she too contributed to this narrative by stating that while she was comfortable working with black students, she was "least comfortable with Asian students." She and the others silently and tacitly agreed with Marcy and the personnel director.

Working with white teachers and my commensurate attempt to engage in the process of breaking down the culture of silence, it became increasingly vital for me as both researcher and participant to pay careful attention to how the layers in a hegemonic discourse inhibited our reception and interpretation of the absences as well as our reactions to what was spoken. To sift through these layers involved confronting the question of purpose or intent latent in the silences or absences as well as attempting to determine the types or categories of silences or absence that might be present.

With such an encounter it is essential not only to consider the meaningful silences voiced by research participants, but to consider our own silences as researchers and how/why we strategically employ such silences. Alisha Waller (2006) in probing her own silent questions, those that are part of her consciousness but that she censors and withholds in her conversations with research participants, writes about how in the process of conducting an interview, she is at the same time questioning her own motives and playing the "what if" questions that she chooses not to ask. Similarly, Laurel Richardson (1997) displays what she terms her "interior monologue" as part of the field notes that she presents in the context of a discussion of ethnographic data in the essay "The Case of the Skipped Line" (p. 158). This interior monologue echoes the silent questions that Waller posits. In the section where Richardson is presenting an excerpt from a conversation, she indicates the spoken words of both herself and the other "characters," but she further includes her interior monologue as part of the discussion/conversation, or at least as part of the conversation that she is considering as she presents and analyzes her findings.

The problematic of silence will encourage us to investigate how we perpetuate sameness, hegemony, or privilege through this interior monologue. This monologue will indicate what we fail to voice in the form of our silent questions or assumptions, the silences that we fail to challenge on the part of our participants, or an absence of the probing of their silent questions. Such a monologue will also point toward what we fail to voice in our encounters with others in the field. We will come to appreciate that even if we fail to consider silence as data because we wish to "fix" meaning, the silences will always be present, some intelligible and others not. As researchers we can choose to ignore the silences, but we cannot prevent them from haunting the discourse.

These strategies take seriously silence as a data source not previously considered as relevant or as informing meaning in a consideration of what constitutes meaning in discourse-based research. In order to move beyond a dismissal of these silences, and as a way to consider the silences not as secondary to the spoken texts provided by our participants but as essential components, as the meaning between words, such strategies rely on a deconstructive methodology. This interplay, or rather *play* of strategy and methodology, is a vital constituent contained within the conceptualization of a problematic of silence that serves to substantiate the recognition and validation of this silence as data in discourse-based research.

In discussing ethnography as a process, LeCompte and Preissle (1993) state, "ethnographic research is holistic. Ethnographers seek to construct descriptions of total phenomena within their various contexts" (p. 3). Silence now can take its place as part of the "total phenomena" with which we work as educational ethnographers using a holistic approach within a poststructuralist paradigm. We will now consider the trace always already present in the silence, or as Spivak (1976) explains in the preface to *Of Grammatology*, to consider the silence not as secondary or adjunct to the primary text, but as an essential element of the primary text. We will now elevate silence beyond an adjunct to the primary text, and to consider as Spivak proposes, how silence inserts itself within the interstices, filling gaps in the conversations, thereby allowing for a holistic interpretation—in other words, to fully examine silence as an element of the total phenomena.

Performative Silences

If, as Maggie MacClure (2003) contends, educational events and situations are texts, what might be learned from an understanding of these events and situations as performances?

Viewed as performances, we can re-imagine the enacting of such conversations in a performative or theatrical context. I am not referring to performance ethnography as discussed by McCall (2000), but in keeping with McCall's historical discussion of performance ethnography, I am distinguishing between "dramatic scripts" (e.g., transcripts and traditional "texts") and "particular productions of them" (e.g., the enacting of conversations with research participants). My emphasis then is not on presenting ethnographic data as a performance, but considering discourse-based data gathered in the field as performance.

Understanding the production of a script by our participants as a performance allows for a deciphering of the silences present in the "lines" recited by our participants. Given such an orientation, the silent specter becomes not just a haunting presence, but a presence that inhabits. As haunting can be understood as "to frequent," it moves us to consider how we might regard silences as frequent visitors, rather than occasional presences, apparitions, or textual silences. Phillip McGuire writes of silences in the plays of William Shakespeare, both those that he terms "open silences," or those that are open to interpretation, perhaps unintelligible, and "intentional or strategic" silences, those silences that are mandated by Shakespeare because the words "given" to the character are those of silence.

> The words that make up what many would call the 'text' of a play by Shakespeare have an authority that cannot be denied. Indeed, without those words, the open silence would not exist. The existence of open silences, however, compels us to acknowledge the limits of textual authority. The words of the text do not provide us with the means—'the authoritative datum'—for understanding the open silences that the words themselves generate. For such understanding we must turn to performances. What we can learn from performances is something other than, something different from, something outside of the knowledge that the text can provide. It is something without which our knowledge of the play is less than complete. (McGuire, 1985, pp. xxiv-xxv)

If we are bound by the textual authority of the printed transcript that we analyze and describe, we are bound as researchers by a knowledge that only the "text" can provide. As such, our consideration of the "play" is less than complete. If our problematic dictates that we consider only the spoken words in the form of the printed transcript in an analysis and representation of our interactions with participants, then we ignore a multiplicity of meanings present in an enactment of the data. In further describing the literary analysis that he employs in understanding the plays of Shakespeare, McGuire asserts that in order to develop a more complete understanding of a Shakespearean playtext, it is necessary to devise "a method that combines close analysis of the words of a Shakespearean playtext with equally rigorous analysis of the details of particular performances arising from that playtext" (p. 122)—in other words, to engage a methodological practice that recognizes the freedom of both the voiced words and performative silences. Such a methodological practice considers as essential the role that we as researchers, as audience, as spectators, play in shaping the way in which the dialogue is delivered and interpreted with each "hearing." A further treatment of this practice will be discussed in Chapters Five, Six, and Seven.

I am not intending to give up on the idea of a "text" constructed from the meaning that we make in our encounters in the field. My desire is to create a text that is informed by more than a reading and rereading of transcripts and to move toward one as described by McCall (2000) in his description of the process for creating an ethnographic performance script (p. 427). This "script" will be crafted through a listening and relistening to the performances present in the audiotaped conversations. Richard Schechner (cited in McGuire, 1985) describes how, with the advent of printing, the focus in theatrical circles shifted from one of an emphasis on the performance to an emphasis on maintaining the integrity of the exact words. With such a shift, the printed words became primary, "how they were said, and what gestures accompanied them, was...of lesser importance" (p. 124). A deconstructive methodology will provide a means of reclaiming those subordinated elements of performance in an analysis of discourse-based data.

"Ultimately, however, the challenge is more than one of methodology. It is, fundamentally, a matter of ontology and epistemology—of determining what a play is and how we can best proceed to know it" (McGuire, p. 122). This insight is consistent with imagining or re-imagining a problematic of silence that seeks to determine what speech is in the context of discourse-based research, and how we can best proceed to acknowledge, hear, and know it.

How then do we proceed to understand what constitutes the "play" enacted in the field? How does a problematic open up for us in terms of developing strategies for "knowing" what is spoken? Returning to Giroux's definition of a problematic, it calls us to pursue what has been left out in the form of the silences in the script. The problematic of silence provides an entrée to what is possible, plausible, knowable, askable, thinkable, considerable, or hearable. It moves us beyond the current circumference of our consideration and invites us to enter that presence that, if listened for, listened to, heard, will lead to a more inclusive understanding of a multiplicity of meanings.

These silences are not containable or predictable, but contribute to a layered understanding of the characters that inhabit the performative sites of our research. It is important to once again emphasize that this is not an attempt to fix a definition of silence, to suggest that all of the silences are intelligible, or even to stipulate those criteria for silences that count. A problematic of silence is intended to open up the space within which silence is no longer considered as secondary to speech, but rather is considered as a communicative tool employed by ourselves as researchers in concert with our participants as we enact our performative roles in the field of the play.[1]

Roguish Data

In Chapter Two play was put into play in such a way as to produce meaningful silences—ones both *play full* and *full of play*. These *playful* silences tease, entice, and break the rules. They are playful in an appealingly bold way as they enact what I fondly refer to as roguish data.[2] These "performative" movements of silence that play, that are allowed to play, that we allow to play as rogues in the sandlot without too many rules, or with made up rules, rather than confining them to the field with uniforms and referees, produce meaning full silences, ones that do, in fact, inflect something other than a dominant voiced interpretation (Derrida, 2005). This "data" cannot be contained; it is playful, it must be allowed to play within the performative, enacted roles which produce those poetic inter-pretations that counter/challenge the dominant interpretation of data, language, and speech.

These rogues do not follow the rules. They will not let us assume that because words are spoken their meaning is more important and more transparent. They will subvert our analy-sis and representation of "data" if we too closely define/confine what is "permissible." Paradoxically if we do entertain these silent rogues, they may repulse us, frighten us, worry us, and at the same time entice us, having much to teach us that just may undo us.

A problematic of silence welcomes these rogues, these ir-ruptions that do not play by the rules. It welcomes those that surprise us, the ones that shake us out of our slumber, the ones that play in the streets, the rascals, the prodigals, the ad-venturers. These are the voices that beckon, the ones that we fear and envy in the same moment, the ones that speak in the darkness of night, that elicit our entry into the world of silence to produce a different voice. They will make themselves known to us in the context of a problematic of silence, and they will speak to us like the voice of the radical poet who masterfully speaks with words, between words, and without words.

CHAPTER 5
A Poetic of Silence

The Voice of the Poet

In our work as researchers, we often focus on data that can be catalogued and named. We focus on the voice of our participants so as to give voice to their experiences, their questions, their oppressions, and their wisdom. What we often fail to do is give voice to the poetic among them, who, like the poets, speak masterfully with words, between words and without words. As spoken by Derrida (1994) "we are inheritors of more than one form of speech, as well as of an injunction that is itself disjointed" (p. 16). If we are to allow these multiple forms of speech to inhabit our field sites and our transcripts, we may encounter the poetic forms that violate our normative expectations of speech because, according to Richardson (1997), the poetic form "plays with connotative structures and literary devices to convey meaning, commends itself to multiple and open readings in ways that straight sociological prose does not" (p. 143).

While as methodologists we may ground ourselves in feminist theory, poststructural theory and deconstruction, claiming a dismantling of the binaries that shape us, we may at the same time fail to notice the preference given to prose, voice and text. As inheritors of an academic culture that has constructed us and that holds authority over us, we are prone to the suppressing and devaluing of these poetic interpretations (Richardson, 1997, p. 147). In this "enlightened negligence," we miss the wisdom and voice offered by a look at the poets who remind us of the use of silence not as a tool, nor an extra, but as an essential element in an understanding of meaning and voice. By employing the tools of layout, punctuation, form and lineation (Lennard, 1996), the poet can purposefully force/create/allow the silences to inhabit the poems with their meaning. The poet suffuses the poem with silence that is both meaning *full* and purpose *full.*

In his discussion of Eugenio Montale's poetry, Clodagh Brook (2002) writes of Montale's use of silence as "an act of revolt against an impoverished linguistic medium." He continues to affirm what I have stated earlier in this text, "silence is not simply the absence or suspension of speech,...but is a multi-faceted phenomenon with expressive power in its own right" (p. 145). Further, he goes on to state that "silence speaks through the syntax of the poems. It is given a voice in the spaces between the words, and in the space which envelops the poem, thus functioning in a concrete way in the text" (p. 151). Again, I am interested not just in the voice of silence, but how silence is voiced through the poetic constructions of our conversations in the form of data/transcripts that can be understood as speech/meaning/text in silence.

Somewhat similarly to a consideration of the interactions in the field with our participants as performances, we may also consider the texts provided by our participants as poetic constructions. Unlike Laurel Richardson (2002), who constructs poetic representations from interviews and interview experiences, I wish to listen to interviews or conversations with research participants *as* poetic constructions, to be present to the pauses and silences inextricably woven into the conversations. Richardson affirmed such a strategy when she commented, "Poetic representation is a viable method for seeing beyond social scientific conventions and discursive practices, and therefore should be of interest to those concerned with epistemological issues and challenges" (p. 877). Drawing on the work of Dennis Tedlock, an oral historian, Richardson emphasized the importance of considering our spoken conversation as more closely resembling poetry than prose. "In American speech, estimates are that about half of the time we are speaking, we are not; we are pausing....Unlike prose, poetry writes in the pauses through the conventions of line breaks, spaces between lines and between stanzas and sections, and for sounds of silence" (p. 879).

In keeping with a deconstructive methodology and urged toward a "shaking up" of conventional understandings by Hélène Cixous (1997/1994), I look more specifically to the literature of poetry, prose, and literary theory for the development of what I term a "poetic understanding of silence" (Mazzei, 2003). This poetic understanding of silence locates what is marginal in an analysis of empirical materials—in other words, what is not spoken, or at least not audibly spoken—and attempts to give preference to both the spoken words *and* the silent breaths. It attempts to give "textual status" (MacLure, 2003) to the words spoken regardless of form. A poetic understanding takes seriously the lessons concealed in the "hesitations" of speech and "listens" to what Terry Eagleton (1983) referred to as the unarticulated subtexts that may be as important as what is articulated through words, both written and spoken (p. 178). It takes seriously the possibility (or rather impossibility) as stated by Barks (in Rumi, 1995), that "words are not important in themselves, but as resonators for a center" (p. 17), and that without the silent words, the words spoken in silence, in between words, without words, meaning is incomplete. It returns to the question as posed by Maggie MacLure (2006), "What does it mean to mean?" and in so doing, revels in an out of joint, "improper writing" (MacLure, 2003, p. 108) that is unfaithful to expectations and that exceeds the meaning that it is supposed to convey.

What I seek in a poetic of silence is an attempt through my strategic deployment of a deconstructive methodology, to invite, encourage and demand that the specters breach the walls of our commonplace way of hearing data in ways that may surprise us out of our dream state. I want to be like Alice in Wonderland, who "had got so much into the way of expecting nothing but out-of-the-way things to happen, that it seemed quite dull and stupid for life to go on in the common way" (Carroll, 1999/1866). I want to listen/hear the conversations voiced through speech, breath and silence, not in dull and accepted ways, but to listen as one does to poetry—to the shape, breath, and impossible hearing that may allow the poetic element in the construction to breathe.

This attitude of expecting "out-of-the-way" things to happen encourages us to go beyond that moment when language or prose or conventional understandings of data fail us. What if, for example, when asked to discuss their racial identity or themselves as having a racial position white teachers are at a loss for words, are without words, or possess inadequate words? It is essential in that moment to listen with an appreciation that the "not to be spoken" thoughts, emotions, or questions may be expressed in the form of a poetic of silence. Audre Lord (1984) wrote of her encounter with poetry as expressing that which was unintelligible and terrifying: "Right now I could name at least ten ideas I would have found intolerable or incomprehensible and frightening, except that they came in dreams and poems....We can train ourselves to respect our feelings and to transpose them into a language so they can be shared" (p. 37). This attention to the language of silence, the poetic of expression, is to listen/hear the longing spoken in pause, the uncertainty spoken in hesitation, the fear spoken in reservation.

A caution to those of us who seek the poetic voice in our data is that we not romanticize this voice and project onto/into it a verse not intended, a verse that we long for, but that we cannot receive. The poetic voice can be seductive, comforting, and playful. It can be used to mask and obfuscate. As in the poems of Charles Bukowski, the poetic voice can also be vulgar, repulsive, and raw. It can evoke images with few words and, as with previous examples, with no words. To romanticize the poetic voice is to hear the words that we want to be spoken by our lover, rather than to hear the words that our lover may be speaking between the breaths, between the smiles, between the sheets. We must always be aware of our power as researchers to construct narratives from the poetic expressions of our participants if we do not sufficiently trouble the complex and competing texts speaking through audible and inaudible poetic expression.

Of course, we must correspondingly trouble with some probity our own poetic constructions. An emphasis on the spoken text encourages a reticence to search for our own silent voice. In the process of reviewing the tapes in my research with white teachers, I realized that I was not parsing my "voice" for the unnoticed racist comments that I might have unknowingly spoken, racist comments that were not hearable/knowable to me speaking from a position of white privilege. I wrote the following in my research journal at the time:

> July 20, 1995
> Transcribing the tapes in which I am also a participant is a humbling experience. Transcribing my words is like listening to someone else speak and wondering if she is going to reveal an underlying racist attitude, or an absence of her own awareness of self as raced.

Missed in this analysis of course were also the unguarded silences, perhaps more revealing than the voiced responses. In my worrying about the "proper" speech, I failed to take note of what was disclosed in the unnoticed or, perhaps more revealing, silent attitudes—the improper speech.

When we are unguarded, much is expressed, both in thought and in silence. As researchers and research participants, we may choose to keep silent because of what it may reveal. In *Specters of Marx*, Derrida (1994) refers to the "visor effect," the effect of "looking without being seen" (p. 7). What are the ways in which our participants hide behind a mask or veil that permits them to speak without being heard, unless of course we recognize those veiled silences masking as words, speaking by keeping silent. These unguarded silences may be revealing because our participants, like us, find security in hiding behind this wall of silence, but they too will be missed if we fail to consider them as text, as voice, as poetically constituting meaning. Our participants, like us, will fail to recognize the specters that reveal unguarded thoughts in the silent speech or the silent writing on the veiled surface of the original spoken word, specters that often speak with the voice of the poet—speaking, sighing, and exclaiming in those guarded/unguarded moments of silent speech.

Listening to these silences as poetic constructions, we can be attentive to the multiple layers in, around, between the text. In so doing, the texts can be "shaken up, breached, disturbed, torn—so that new questions and meaning are generated" (Mac-Lure, 2003, p. 81). Returning then to the idea of prosody, we analyze not the text in the form of the spoken/written text, but the text in the form of the meter, the rhythm, the break, the sigh, the words and meanings spoken in the unnamed and veiled silences. We catch a glimmer of the previously unconsidered connections and words allowing the poetry spoken in our research encounters to speak that which was previously unthought. We listen to the heartbeat of the poetic voice and within its pulsating rhythm discover the "out of the way things" that breach the walls of the ordinary.[1]

The Art of Listening/Hearing/Speaking

If we are to seriously engage the spoken conversations in our recorded and observed encounters as poetry, then we can perhaps move beyond a reading/hearing of these texts as merely a collection of words, and instead as a collection of sounds, both audible and silent, both spoken and breathed, that contribute to its meaning. Adrienne Rich (1993) offers the following:

> What poetry is made of is so old, so familiar, that it's easy to forget that it's not just the words, but polyrhythmic sounds, speech in its first endeavors (every poem breaks a silence that had to be overcome), prismatic meanings lit by each other's light, stained by each others' shadows. In the wash of poetry the old, beaten, worn stones of language take on colors that disappear when you sieve them up out of the streambed and try to sort them out. (p. 84)

A poetic listening to research texts attempts to reclaim the colors not discernible under the microscope, to attend to the subtle hues and colors of silent breath, of poetic speech, of improper writing, of flowing words. A poetic listening takes seriously (in a Derridean playful sort of way) the fact that a text does not have clear boundaries or rigid forms, just as poetry has no clear boundaries or rigid forms. To note the competing tendencies in the text is not to deny the dominating tendencies in the text, but to allow a space for what else is "echoing" with a softer, more subtle voice. Given such an understanding (or mis-understanding of text), analysis of transcript or conversation, "involves much more than attending to whatever is 'in' those texts" (MacLure, 2003, p. 43) and becomes much more concerned with what is "not" in the texts, or rather what is not in the texts in the way of discernible, fixed boundaries.

Talk to many teachers of poetry, poets, or students of poetry and you will learn that the experience of reading poetry, while important and enjoyable, does not allow for the fullness of that poetry. By that I mean that to silently read the words of a poem is to focus on the text of the poem in the form of the words of the poem—in other words, to focus on the static, containable, knowable sense of "the poem." To hear a poem or to recite a poem is to hear (speak) the breaths, pauses, and emptiness without which a poem reverts to merely being a sequence of words. To speak a poem is to hear the presence in the absence, to feel the cadence in our breath elided when focusing on the "text" as written. From the poem "Where Everything is Music," Rumi (1995, p. 35) captures this idea:

> Poems reach up like spindrift and the edge
> of driftwood along the beach, wanting!
>
> They derive
> from a slow and powerful root
> that we can't see.
>
> Stop the words now.
> Open the window in the center of your chest,
> and let the spirits fly in and out.

Craig Dworkin (2003) in the book *Reading the Illegible* writes of awakening into, not out of a dream. What if we are to consider the conversations in the field as poetic constructions so as to provide a fissure for awakening into silence, or what some might consider the illegible. To awaken out of the promise of spoken and written text as that magical place where meaning resides into a dream that allows silence, breath, pause, absence, and poetry to play. In *The Language of Life*, Bill Moyers (1995) writes of his experience of awakening into this silent dream of poetry:

> When I was a schoolboy our teachers required us to memorize po-
> ems. By copying the lines over and over, I excelled at the sport. But
> it was only sport. The words I had committed to memory were di-
> vorced from meaning or emotions. I knew the poems but not the ex-
> perience of them. Only later, when a series of English teachers gifted
> in Elizabethan theatrics began to read serious poetry aloud in class,
> did I hear the music and encounter the Word within the words. (p.
> xi)

What I seek to claim in a listening to the poetic constructions spoken by research participants and also myself is a listening that breathes life into the empty "words" out of context.
In the following section, I present a discussion of how this poetic understanding of silence began to open up a space for data
that had previously been ignored, discounted, overlooked, and
thus to speak and inform my "textual" analysis. In the following chapter, I further explore how a deconstructive listening
created space for these poetic constructions to cavort with the
specters and how previously missed meanings began to emerge
in the process.

A Poetic Understanding of Silence

As informed by the above discussion, the importance of attending to a poetic understanding of silence is to attend to how
it shapes/changes the way that we speak and the way we listen. Perhaps as importantly, an attending to a poetic understanding of silence is also to attend to the text of our data as a
poetically constructed one (Richardson, 1997) that not only
makes use of poetic convention to craft meaning, but relies on
such convention to communicate. In other words, it depends
on the inclusion of breaths, pauses, spaces, gaps and silences,
to frame and to say what is spoken. Ultimately as researchers,
the importance is to contemplate how this poetic understanding shapes/changes the way we consider data, what counts as
data, and how to attend to such, as was delineated in a discussion of a problematic of silence in Chapter Four.

LeCompte and Preissle (1993) write, "Qualitative researchers must balance between two problems: too much data and
too little data. If the data are too thin, the researcher has in-

sufficient evidence to substantiate results" (p. 54). With the early analysis of the conversations with this group of white teachers, I questioned whether what I had gathered was in fact "thin data." Further examination, however, began to suggest that what I was faced with was not "thin data," but rather an inherited limitation implied in a conventional understanding of the doing of research. In other words, I was constrained within the boundaries of what had traditionally been considered to count as "data." An attachment to my learned understanding of "data" had predisposed me to focus on what was perceived as the primary text (spoken word) rather than a consideration of empirical materials that transgressed traditional boundaries. Elizabeth St. Pierre (1997) in a probing of the unobtrusive traces of data sources maintains that "we have barely begun to name, describe, and account for such in our research" (p. 10). In a more purposeful pursuit of the unobtrusive traces of empirical materials I was less restricted in what I could now consider as possible research sources; therefore silence became a transgressive source of information, one possible for me if I left the restricted notion of data as what we can see, hear and read.

The process for listening to silence did not conform to the conventional constraints imposed in a traditional analysis and interpretation of empirical materials. Nor did it conform to a traditional method of interviewing as being "primarily dependent on spoken text as the basis from which knowledge...would be constructed" (Nairn, Munro & Smith, 2005, p. 223). Listening to silence didn't "happen" as observation in the way we as researchers, or at least this researcher, had been trained to gather and analyze empirical materials but instead was revealed over time, and was a result of careful, patient listening, both during and after the conversations. This empirical material was not always observable or immediately "present," but rather was discovered in the hidden, the covert, the inarticulate: the gaps within/outside the observable. As I have suggested, such awareness was enhanced by the study of silence and its effective use in the realm of literature, especially that of poetry, where the page, the space, the arrangement of word, phrase, gap, breath, all serve to speak, to engage the reader/listener at all levels of expression present in the work.

Adrienne Rich (1993) stated, "We go to poetry because we believe it has something to do with us. We also go to poetry to receive the experience of the *not me*, enter a field of vision we could not otherwise apprehend" (p. 85). I go to poetry because it allows me as a researcher to enter a field of hearing that I could not otherwise conceive of or comprehend.

This process of listening that unfolded was not a desperate attempt to make something out of nothing, or more accurately to fatten up "thin" empirical materials; rather it was a means of research grounded in a persistent belief, affirmed by experience, that as researchers we need to be carefully attentive to what is not spoken, not discussed, not answered, not recited, for in those absences is where the very "fat" and rich information is yet to be known and understood. This "fat" material requires our listening differently and to begin recognizing the richness in our own, and others' silences. Just as "Poetry, in its own way, is a carrier of the sparks, because it too comes out of silence, seeking connection with unseen others" (Rich, 1993, p. 57), then my engagement with the poetic constructions of conversations in the context of research provides a connection and validation between the spoken and silent texts.

Like Laurel Richardson (1993), I am interested in the merits of poetry and prose in qualitative research. Unlike Richardson, I am interested in probing what is to be found in silence using poetry and prose, not as a genre for presenting qualitative research, but as a filter through which to understand metaphors present and absent in the conversations, or as Eagleton would urge, to recognize the importance in the blindnesses and absences. I do not propose a discussion of the silencing of voices, but instead the silence present *in* the narrative voice. I seek the wisdom afforded through a careful examination of the insights present in the blindnesses, absences, and voids; the absences and silences that Maxine Greene (1993) tells us "are as much a part of our history as the articulate voices" (p. 14). I posit the question of how to account for nothingness, absence, or silence as deliberate in an analysis of empirical materials. I strive to create processes or strategies that will serve to facilitate our hearing the voices within the silence.

Attempting this methodological project and informed by a poetics of silence, I began to listen to (or rather listen for) the attempts of our group to articulate a white self in relation to a nonwhite Other. What began to surface were gaps in the conversations, silences that began to speak. These silences, or gaps in the narrative, were a result of our inability to articulate answers because we were either masking the consequences of our blindness or we were unwilling to face the offending presence of our complicity in norming whiteness, similar in some ways to what Russel y Rodríguez (1998) describes as how normative stances contribute to a silencing praxis in anthropology. What emerged as I continued to listen to the group conversations was an awareness, often discovered after the fact, that answers to particularly difficult race-oriented questions tended to be expressed in two ways. One, the response was "comfortable," meaning it was the answer that was congruent with one's self-perception, which, of course, presented the irony that such self-perception did not include the descriptor "white." Secondly, or alternatively, the response was in fact no response, that is to say, it did not address in any substantive manner the question posed. In both types of response there was an articulation of silence, a stated presence, hidden yet manifest in the very act of eliding, denying, or conforming to an unspoken norming presence. These silences, gaps, voids, which I continued to encounter led me to probe their meaning, their expression within the methodology of qualitative research—a design, if you will, which would help to articulate a problematic of silence, specifically grounded in discourse-based research.

To consider our texts then as poetic constructions is to experience the fullness to be found within the texts. It is to savor the pregnant breaths and pauses—the words between words. It is to engage an analysis that limits words not just to letters on a page, or utterances spoken, but as texts that do not conform to a specific hierarchy (Frey, 1996, p. 142). To focus only on the words is to understand what is "said-in-the talk," and is therefore to understand the talk only "approximately and superficially" (Heidegger, 1962b/1927, p. 212). We can have a confidence in what is said, not because it enables a nuanced or full expression, but only "because it is in the same averageness that we have a common understanding of what is said" (p.

212). Such a confidence is only remotely possible if we are to focus on what is said in the fullness of the poetic text.

A Poetic Reading

> Poems allow us to savor a single image, a single phrase....It slows you down to read a poem. You read it more than one time. You read it more slowly than you would speak to someone in a store. And we need that slow experience with words. (Naomi Shihab Nye quoted in Moyers, 1995, p. xvi)

A view of our data as poetic constructions, as poetry, as poems, elicits a reading that permits a slow experience with words. A poetic reading of our data, data as poetry, conversations as poetic constructions, may lead us to listening and recitation practices that change/shape our interactions with our data in the same way that our relationship to a poem changes with its recitation. How we elide the words on the page in the same way that we elide the silences, breaths and absences that speak in the interstices of the audibly voiced may become known to us, resulting in a tapping into the sensory experience of voice that renders the words within and between words as meaning full.

Such a reading changes our relationship to the text and to its possible meanings in productive ways. In fact, Hans-Jost Frey (1996) encourages such constant examination of and repositioning of our relationship to the text. "You could almost say that we get closest to a text when our relationship to it seems most endangered. Finding and losing are close bedfellows in reading. The most important discovery is all the closer the less we can firmly hold onto it" (p. 2).

As we read a poem, recite a poem, and read it again, the emphasis on words, syllables, and pauses can shift from one moment to the next. Such a poetic encounter points us toward a deconstructive reading filled with multiple and competing voices, those that are silent, whispered, or spoken. It relies on the excess of the text that overflows with all that is not said. It seeks the barely perceptible specter, the silent ghost, and incites a "craving for the cloud of unknowing beyond knowledge and for the silence beyond speech" (Sontag, 1991/1969, pp. 4–5). It invites a deconstructive methodology that no longer seeks to constrain the multiple and competing voices, but contains them within the circumference of what is now audible—those voices that speak with silent whispers.

CHAPTER 6
Silent Listenings: Deconstructive Practices

The Possible Made *Impossible*

In Chapter Two I put forward that the only possible invention of a deconstructive methodology is impossible, and for that reason, it is the only conceivable method. It is the only conceivable method because those methods bound by what is possible can no longer contain the multiple and competing voices, those that are silent, whispered, or spoken. Again, this does not indicate a move on my part to give up on data, or meaning, or understanding, rather, as with any push toward the limits of our current problematics, a deconstructive methodology acknowledges and engages lessons from a research tradition that has shaped current practices as I attempt to work both within and against those lessons learned. Derrida (1997) confirms this when stating:

> The paradox in the instituting moment of an institution is that, at the same time that it starts something new, it also continues something, is true to the memory of the past, to a heritage, to something we receive from the past, from our predecessors, from the culture.... That is what deconstruction is made of: not the mixture but the tension between memory, fidelity, the preservation of something that has been given to us, and, at the same time, heterogeneity, something absolutely new, and a break. (p. 6)

In the preceding chapters I presented a conceptualization of a deconstructive methodology as a strategy toward opening up the binaries and the boundaries of data, speech, voice, and meaning in order to "hear" that which has been previously discounted, disregarded, or unobserved. It is important now to show how this deconstructive methodology can be "put to work" in the doing of qualitative research. This "putting to work" hearkens to the call by researchers in the social sciences (e.g., Lather, 2004; Peters & Burbules, 2004; Spivak, 1999) that in order for poststructural theory to be relevant, working examples of the applications of such theory in educational research must be presented as exemplars.

As I also indicated in the earlier chapters, since there is no secret, no single meaning, no one "right way" to hear and analyze our data, it would seem that my pursuit of and use of deconstructive strategies to be found in a deconstructive methodology would appear to be the most plausible means by which the voice of those restless specters of silence that circulate in and through the text can lay claim to our attention. They playfully invite us to "overcome the extreme rationalism of technological language" (Caputo, 1986, p. 172) and listen differently—more purposefully, more attentively, more closely, even, yes, irrationally—so that we and our participants alike can hear the voices both within and between words.

Answers Between Words

In the social science research that engages issues of social justice, much is written and espoused regarding the Other—how we exoticize the Other, speak for the Other, marginalize the Other, etc. What is the Other in our research practice? Is the Other that which we fear? Is the Other perhaps the words between words—full of meaning but unpredictable? Do we shun this Other for more solid ground in our data?

In work with white teachers regarding their relationship with race, what I came to hear (*finally*) was that much was being spoken that was not being heard. I had fallen into the trap that any good poststructuralist vehemently denies—that of creating a binary, in my case a binary of spoken text and silent emptiness. This silence was experienced as absent of meaning; it was not voiced so was therefore Other to my purpose. Derrida (1994/1993) insists that "we are inheritors of *more than one* form of speech" (p. 16), and yet there was no acknowledgment on my part of being an inheritor of this Other "not spoken" speech. While embracing heterogeneity in my research focus, I was denying heterogeneity in my consideration of text and thus reinscribing the binary once again. There was no openness to the Other of data, to the fact that "heterogeneity opens things up, it lets itself be opened up by the very effraction of that which unfurls, comes, and remains to come— singularly from the other" (p. 33).

The need, of course, was to loose myself from the extreme rationalism of spoken language, voiced text, tangible data, such that I might finally be capable of a movement "beyond the opposition between presence and non-presence, actuality and inactuality, life and non-life, of thinking the possibility of the specter, the specter as possibility" (Derrida, 1994, p. 12). In other words, in order to "hear" the silence of my text as presence, as spoken, as possible, there was the need for the *impossible* of a deconstructive methodology.

A Context for Silence

The records of research that prompted (playfully invited) me to consider the possibility of this elusive specter were primarily obtained through group interaction, thus making critical the need to present as accurately as possible participant response in the form of conversations. These conversations were not closed-ended interviews, as they did not rely on a format dictated by a prescribed interview guide (Bogdan & Biklen, 1992), nor were they focus groups, as I did not function as an objective facilitator who refrained from providing an opinion (Templeton, 1994). They were carried out in an open-ended format that allowed "an interviewee-guided investigation of a lived experience" (Reinharz, 1992, p. 21). The content of our conversations did not ensue from the specific questions of an "interview" but rather the focus of each session grew from assigned readings and the reflections by each participant between meetings. In the early stages of these conversations I had very few prepared questions thereby allowing the discussion to revolve around questions or comments made by group

members which served as a means of further facilitating inquiry and insight into our shared experience as white teachers
(Holstein & Gubruim, 1995, pp. 46-47).

In his presentation of four phases toward methodological
sophistication in research interviewing, Charles Briggs (1986)
wrote about the importance of "reflexivity in the interviewing
process" (p. 100) and suggested periodic analysis considering a
variety of factors including the respondent, interviewer, social
roles of those participating, and their social situation. This
analysis serves to indicate how these factors function collec-
tively and independently to shape the meaning of what is being
said (p. 101). In heeding Briggs's advice, I engaged in a reflexive analysis during the early phase of my project and it did
prove instructive, but it also served to limit my understandings
and interpretations.

My weekly review of the group transcripts was necessary as
I was meeting with this group of teachers for multiple sessions,
and during those reviews I sought to identify questions or responses to revisit in subsequent conversations (Reinharz,
1992, p. 36). In that process I was quite intent on what each
person was saying and how it was being said—so intent, in
fact, that I was not cognizant at the time of what was being left
out. This treatment of conversational analysis was certainly
consistent with the assertion by Elinor Ochs (1979) that "In
nearly all linguistic, sociological, and psychological treatments
of adult-adult speech behavior, nonverbal considerations in
the immediate situation are minimized or ignored" (p. 52). I
was certainly being reflexive, but I was also failing to attend to
how the social situation of the speaker might be communicat-
ing more in the pauses and silences than in the speech. One of
the women in the group could be candid in her collective description of the black students in her school, yet reticent to
answer questions asked by a male member of the group that
urged her to consider how such a description might be considered racist. The specters were certainly at play but the voice of
their silence was still quite muffled.

As these conversations were not "conventional," my attempts to record, transcribe, code, and analyze them conven-
tionally also proved to be problematic. The stories begged for a
more nuanced interpretation than, say, a realist tale format

could provide (see, e.g., Van Maanen, 1988). Again prompted by Briggs (1986), my questions were becoming more probing with greater adeptness of timing, but even so, the critical moment of experiencing how to *listen* had yet to be achieved.

Briggs suggests "perhaps the most basic maxim to be followed is that the interview must be analyzed as a whole before any of its component utterances are interpreted" (p. 104)—in other words, to let the narratives speak in the fullness of their context. But to truly let the narratives "speak" there was needed a different approach not just for listening, but also for *hearing* these conversations. It became readily apparent that such an approach was not waiting to be pulled from the shelf and hurried into action. No, the realization was neither to be obvious nor planned, but rather one forged in a continuing struggle with the doing of qualitative research *within* a post-structuralist paradigm and *against* a postpositivist paradigm.

My analysis of the conversations continued using a traditional approach consisting of reading through the transcripts while identifying the themes present and creating categories by which the data could be separated and sorted (Huberman & Miles, 1994). But slowly (ever so slowly) this separating and sorting created a troubling resistance. Simply reading the transcribed verbatim narratives was proving inadequate both from a cognitive/analytical assessment and from an emotive/experiential engagement. The voice modulations of the speakers were lost, as were the pauses, the sighs, and the significance of each (Scheurich, 1995). The absences *in* the narratives had become absent *from* the narratives.

Now that the resistance within the text (those playful specters again?) had gotten my attention, it became ever more evident that, more than just "listening" to the text, it was of critical importance to "hear" the text, those nuances and meanings present in the modulated voices, the absences, the silences, both intentional and unintentional. Putting aside the printed transcripts I returned to the oral record; in other words, I listened again to the taped conversations. Gradually the absences (or what had been experienced as absence) wove their way into the "spoken text" and allowed a seductive intimation of themselves as altogether different voices, those meanings present in the absence that were not yet ready to be "analyzed" but that could now at least be heard. And within this fresh encounter with the empty space of silence was found a presence that was camouflaged as an absence. Often this absence or silence was a nonresponse to a question. It was not that the participants didn't "speak" to queries, but rather they gave responses to different questions than those that had been posed.

In questions regarding racial identity, for example, individuals would couch their responses in how they saw themselves in relation to a non-white Other. On one such occasion, a lengthy conversation ensued about how the women in the group reacted when encountering a black male on the street at night or in an elevator. Another "nonresponse" response was related to a discussion of white privilege. Instead of a critical examination of how "white" is privileged (as presented in an article by Peggy McIntosh, 1990) and how this privilege affects one's perception of white in relation to the Other, the conversation focused on what whites enjoy by virtue of their privileged position as whites. Even the idea of "white" as privileged was resisted by some of the participants, who suggested rather that the McIntosh article we had read was several years old and "surely" most of those "privileges" had been erased in the time that had elapsed. The specters in their absent presence were jumping for joy within, around and outside the text. Their presence cried out for the "impossible" hearing possible with a deconstructive method, but the veil had not yet been lifted.

The silences and absences in these conversations, both intentional and unintentional, were indeed spoken behind a veil. They were masked in this case by a lack of awareness of white as a racial category or the lack of desire to see white as a racial category. This failure or intent produced a response, a nonresponse, a spoken silence bound within a myopia that resisted seeing the Self as Other, that resisted seeing oneself as being seen. Such a resistance is in itself a "speech act" full of meaning and essential to an understanding and analysis of the text. Just as a male participant in the group made the remark, "I'm wondering how valid some of these [privileges] are and whether I'm getting it," we as qualitative researchers must ask how valid the silent absences are and whether or how we are getting it.

As Cixous (2001/1998) puts forth, our veils can serve to mask what we choose not to see, or wish not to see, for to see is sometimes unbearable. "Not-seeing-oneself is a thing of peace" (p. 12). By looking through a veil of whiteness, for example, we can avoid what is invisible and unknowable. Answering a question other than the one posed, as illustrated by Derrida (2002), results in a deflection that, although often not intentional, is purposeful nonetheless and must be considered as critical in our understanding of the data.

The silences are not always veiled nor are they always unintentional, but they can often be deliberate and purposeful—a choosing not to speak or speaking with veiled words. A young woman in a class that I was teaching when given a choice to write an article reflection on one of four selections had this to say about the essay by James Baldwin, "A Talk to Teachers." "When I first read this article, I immediately said I would not write a reflection on this one. It was too touchy, too controversial, and I did not want to get involved. I read the article and moved on. I read the other articles and none of them touched me like this one did...What was I afraid of? I knew I wasn't afraid to talk about race, about teaching, so why was I afraid to talk about race *and* teaching?" One of the women in my study stated: "I have very different views than many people do and I don't like confrontations so I usually keep my opinions to myself." The commensurate experience of another female participant was: "These issues [race] have always been kept quiet. I tend to just sit and take things in, and if I do speak I am afraid that I will offend someone who may be sensitive to the issue." Another echoed, "Sometimes I am afraid of using a slang term or idea that might offend others." These participants, and as is often the case with students in my classes, intentionally hesitated or paused, or didn't speak for fear of "saying the wrong thing." A silent voice was evoked to avert calling attention to oneself, to avoid exposing what was beneath the veil, especially if in speaking they risked revealing having become more like the Other. An intentional silence was induced that fulfilled the desire not to be perceived as different, (Other), or impolite, or perhaps even racist. The result was that they re-produced their own whiteness through a resolute silence.

Ruth Frankenberg (1996) wrote of her recognition that whiteness was present in her life, but was not spoken. "Whiteness seemed not to be named, as far as memory tells me. Odd really, since there was so much of it about" (p. 5). Whiteness is all around us, but because it is so prevalent, it is seen by whites as normative and therefore not named. Further, Frankenberg (1993) proposed that "for many white people in the United States...'color-blindness'—a mode of thinking about race organized around an effort to not 'see,' or at any rate not to acknowledge, race differences—continues to be the 'polite' language of race" (p. 142). Because, as Frankenburg (1996) told her students, "race privilege is the (non)experience of not being slapped in the face" (p. 4), whites very often are not called to consider their whiteness as a racial position. This failure to consider one's own racial positioning, coupled with a cultural taboo learned early by many whites that it is impolite to notice color or difference, produces silences that are meaning full.

What became increasingly evident and decisive in these conversations was the importance of this silent speech in an understanding of how these teachers coded, veiled, and privileged their whiteness. When Janet, a preservice teacher states "I never thought about the fact that I'm white until the black students at my school made it an issue," and even though this whiteness was pointed out to her by her black students, she went on to assert, "In my daily life now, I never give it a second thought." It is not necessary for her to give it a second thought because she does not have to, and because to do so is to acknowledge her privilege. Elizabeth Ellsworth (1997) wrote of this silence present when whites do notice their positioning and "keep silent" to fit in with acceptable (normative) "white" behavior and attitudes. The silent speech that she described was present in the nonresponses, evasions, and rationalizations of the teachers. It was present in Janet's speaking about her white privilege by not speaking about it. It was present in the hesitations, pauses, and resistances. It was present in every act of speaking. This silent speech was both purposeful and meaningful, therefore necessitating that a methodological strategy be devised to facilitate my hearing what was being spoken within this "silent speech."

A Process for Listening

I had heard the stories twice. First with the initial conversations and the listening that occurred as participants replied in response to my questions, comments, and those of the other group members. The second listening occurred in the process of "rehearing" while transcribing the tapes. I then reread the transcription after each session in preparation for the next group meeting. I had considered listening to the tapes a third time, even marking words that were stressed and noting pauses as a valuable practice, but at the time I only understood this potential value as a means to further refine and "validate" the "data" rather than as a process for becoming more familiar with the narrative (Glesne, 1999, pp. 31-33).

One of my peer reviewers remarked that, by the time she began to write the analysis section of her study, she had practically memorized her tapes, having identified important issues while knowing "who said what." She had established an intimacy through listening to her tapes that I realized I had not achieved through reading and analyzing my transcripts.[1] How was I to establish intimacy with the conversations of my participants in the absence of their voices? How was I to minimize the misunderstandings and misplaced meanings that occur during the process of translation, in this case, the process of transcription?

The thought of listening to my tapes as a way to live with the narratives had not occurred to me. This would mean listening to the tapes numerous times and developing a process for listening to allow me to untangle the layers, the complexities, and the contradictions to be found there. I needed to cultivate a method of reflexive listening (Denzin, 2002) that would allow me to hear the narratives previously elided.

To cultivate this method, I began by listening to the tapes while reading along with the transcripts. Listening to the tapes, like listening to poetry, served to retard the pace of reading, thus encouraging further thoughts and reflections and a greater intimacy with the narrative. When I had initially read the transcripts without listening, my tendency had been to read quickly as one does to "get through" a massive amount of material in a short amount of time. When read in this manner,

nuance was often elided as I was being attentive only to the
words that were spoken, not to *how* they were spoken. On listening to the tapes while reading along with the transcripts,
greater attention was paid to the conversation in context, noting its ebb and flow and thus "analyzing" the stories in situ or
in their original narrative form. Paying attention to the voice
modulations of the speakers, as well as to the pauses and
sighs, I began to ascertain the significance of each. Nervous
laughter in response to a query about how you choose to describe yourself has meaning, a meaning lost in the one-
dimensional world of the transcript.

Subsequently, I listened without reading the transcripts. As
I heard phrases that intrigued me or as I was prompted to ask
a question, I would note these thoughts, letting them pass as
ink flowing on paper, much as one lets thoughts escape and
flow when in a meditative state. This way of listening enabled
me to hear the absences, the pauses, and the whispers, much
as one experiences and "hears" the rests and the pauses in
music. When one of the women described her friends and her
different lifestyle as compared with her family, she was always
dancing on the edge of saying what she meant. I knew that she
was in a relationship with a black male, but her descriptions to
the group were teeming with those silent specters. They were
again playfully jumping up and down and screaming "here we
are" when she stated, "I've come to a very open-minded understanding as far as my friends, as far as people who I go out on
dates with...and its very, *very* conflicting with my parents.
[How?] You know, I want to do things with the person that I'm
going out with right now and it's wrong [Why?] and I'm thinking, you know what's the difference if I get along with somebody or if my friend is Hispanic, or you know, [no, we don't
know, tell us] what's the big deal." Yes, what was the big deal
that prompted the pause, the silence, or the omission, both on
her part, and also in the bracketed questions that we as group
members hesitated to ask? This absent presence in the narrative begs for a hearing; it is the voice that is so often "unheard"
or discounted or the receptacle of our projections as we "fill in"
the blanks with what we are comfortable hearing. After listening with this "blank slate" (my tablet, not my mind), I reviewed
the transcripts and field notes being particularly attentive to

my written comments in an attempt to develop an organizational framework that might guide me in listening to the tapes once again.

This final strategy was undertaken as an intent to hear with an ear to the *multiple* layers of meaning present in the conversations. At this stage, the *process* of listening was more important than the *product* of listening. Present were layers within which the pauses breathed deeply and the silences were given voice. Present also were responses (absences) that had been dismissed as a failure to respond when in fact they were purposeful responses. During this hearing of the tapes the silence revealed its incipient importance as both purposeful and meaningful in discourse-based research. One woman in the group described the "orientation" she was given by the personnel director for the district before her first year teaching in a predominantly African American school. The advice given was, "Your classroom is going to be noisy, they don't sit still, they're verbal learners...don't give them a worksheet, they won't even read it, etc." The woman went on to say that the personnel director was right. No one in the group challenged her assumptions or behavior. Instead, the conversation affirmed that the members believed that they had been given a lot of information about how to work with black students, but that little information was possessed by the group members as to how to work with Asian students.

Why did no one challenge these essentializing narratives? Did the other members hold the same assumptions? Were they afraid of pointing out the initial speaker's racist attitudes for fear of their own complicity? Did they not see this as a racist approach? "Just as conversations can jointly produce collective memories, so, too, they can accomplish denials and projections, as speakers combine to move talk away from tabooed topics, jointly protecting what cannot be uttered. In this way, the unsayable will be present, even if marked by its absence" (Billig, 1997, p. 151).

What emanated from the narrative by using this listening strategy was a strong presence of those silences previously not heard. In discussing models of narrative, Danow (1997) said that in our negative expressions of silence in relation to spoken narrative we relegate silence to an absence or nonoccurrence of utterance. In fact, our obsession with the *word* often causes us to overlook what is articulated in the absence of speech, or *silent speech*. If we engage the silences as meaningful and purposeful, we will "hear" thoughts and meanings previously considered unuttered, unstated, and therefore unintelligible. While some of the silences may in fact be unintelligible, they are nonetheless meaning full. The questions raised in the above paragraph are important and should be raised, but as important or perhaps more important is an encounter with the silence that permeates our narratives. How that silence can serve to camouflage in our silent collusion or to enlighten in our attentiveness is the incisive effect of a deconstructive methodology.

This silence is often a literal absence, but just as often it is an intended unintended silence. In an address at the University of Virginia, Derrida (2002) claimed speech in silence. Although he was more deliberate and intentional about this silence than we often are in conversation with others, the results are the same. "Because I would rather not simply remain silent about what I should have spoken to you about, I will say a word about it in the form of an excuse. I will speak to you, then, a little about what I will not speak to you about and about what I would have wanted—because I ought—to have spoken about" (p. 46). None of my participants would have phrased their "silence" in quite that manner but in fact they (we) often "speak to you about what I will not speak to you about." Our (my) obsession with the spoken word renders us deaf to that "silent speech," what "ought to be spoken about." We can be left insensible to the voices and meanings inhabiting the intentional and unintentional silences. By moving from a focus on the *product* of listening to one centered in the *process* of listening, we can lift this intractable veil and allow the silent speech to be amplified.

Consistent with the experience of Dunbar, Rodriguez, and Parker (2002), my research project also affirmed that interview research exploring race and subjectivity can result in some respondents remaining silent or inarticulate on race. It is not that they have nothing to say, but that their silences have alternative explanations (p. 287). "The result is that the sensitive and astute researcher tries to look past and into the silences that greet interview questions in order to understand the possible categorical sources of silence" (p. 289). This recognition of the presence of the silences leads to a listening for those silences as well as ways and means of hearing them. Of course there were and continue to be unintelligible silences that are perhaps purposeful but not readily discernible. Just as post-structuralist theory has disclaimed the transparency of language, so too does an exploration of silence disclaim that all silences can be knowable. Yet, in the possible impossible of a deconstructive methodology, strategies present themselves which irrupt the boundaries of discourse-based research and by allowing us to step outside, to be within and without, we are given greater possibility to hear the voices of those specters of the absent presence.

Voices of the Specters

In this culture of silence in my work with the group of white teachers, it became evident that rather than one "silence," there were multiple silences. What was I hearing in these silent breaths? How were these absences attempting to make themselves known? It was important to discern and articulate the various voices with which they spoke. There were silences that were polite or comfortable silences: thoughts not spoken for fear of offense. There were silences grounded in a white privilege that often precluded awareness of white as a racial category: a cultural blindness or "white-out" if you will. There were silences that were veiled: intending to conceal or at least muffle racist thoughts or actions. There were silences that were intentional: a choosing not to speak. And of course there were silences that were unintelligible: perhaps purposeful but not readily discernible. These "categories of silence" served to clarify the various voices within a problematic of silence. They do not function as a checklist or as a heuristic by which researchers can listen for these "categories" but rather to consider how the data that I was reviewing had much to say in the silent pronouncements.

Polite Silences. "If you can't say something nice, don't say anything at all" was an admonition many of us received from our parents growing up. I have found this to be an important script as I work with preservice teacher education students, consistent also with my experiences in this research project. As whites, many of us are afraid of calling attention to race (especially our own) because we do not wish to be seen as uncaring, insensitive, or racist. When speaking of her silence in the multicultural education class, one of the women remembered, "At the end of the class I was afraid to say anything. I was afraid to say anything in that class because I didn't know...the right word." A doubting of how her remarks might be interpreted by others induced a polite silence, a desire not to be perceived as antagonistic or impolite, or worse, racist.

The participants in my study often revealed a hesitancy to speak for fear of offending someone. In this fear of offending, we say nothing, we are silent. As articulated by another group member, "When we talk about the whole issue of language and political correctness...if we make things sound nice it means that everything's nice." My students in preservice teacher education classes often indicate a reluctance to speak for fear of offending someone, particularly when the discussion shifts to race and ethnicity. These examples seem not only to suggest but also to affirm that polite silences are both intentional and purposeful.

Privileged Silences. In preparation for one of our group meetings we agreed to read the Peggy McIntosh (1990) article "White Privilege: Unpacking the Invisible Knapsack." Our reading led to a subsequent discussion questioning the validity of statements or privileges that McIntosh asserts are invisible to whites by the very fact that they are rendered invisible by whiteness. "I'm curious about people's reactions," asks one participant. "I'm wondering how valid some of these are and whether I'm getting it." Because as whites we do not have to attend to difference or because we are able to choose to do so, white privilege remains elusive, unintelligible, and silent. If we don't agree that we experience privilege, or are unable to identify this privilege, then we are also unable to speak about this privilege.

We don't "get it," referencing the statement above, when we speak from a position of privilege that affords us the luxury of not even considering the question of whiteness and it's attendant advantages unless we choose to do so. Perhaps more importantly, unless it is pointed out to us, we can avoid participation in the conversation. Even then, we are reluctant to admit that we enjoy such privilege because it is the lens through which we filter the world around us.

Another troublesome issue for the group was McIntosh's use of the word "privilege." A dictionary definition states that privilege is a special advantage, immunity, permission, right, or benefit granted to or enjoyed by an individual, a class, or a caste. Particularly if whites perceive themselves as "victims" of reverse discrimination, this notion of privilege is difficult for them to accept. Even if they don't see themselves as victims, they have never lived without the attendant advantages of white privilege and therefore have difficulty viewing the advantages they enjoy as being attributable to skin color. A failure to accept the concept of whiteness as privilege further perpetuates a desire to validate the privilege, thus privileged silences result. As humans, we breathe air without a constant reminder that the invisible gas is what sustains our breath. If removed or polluted, it becomes painfully visible just as a consideration of whiteness or privilege is not knowable until it is pointed out, challenged, and perhaps removed. If acknowledged, this privilege can become painfully visible. If not acknowledged, it continues to provide a veil through which vision is clouded.

Veiled Silences. Early in the research project, I asked the participants two questions. The first was to generate a list of adjectives they would use to describe themselves to someone they don't know. The second was to talk about their racial identity. A very interesting thing that happened in both instances was that there was an absence of whiteness or of race talk. As whites, we don't describe ourselves as white: it is the norm, it is a given, and therefore a silence occurs. We describe ourselves as learners, as Jews and Christians, even as men and women, but it rarely occurs to us to include white as one of the descriptors.

When I posed a series of questions that I hoped would initiate a discussion of our place as whites in the racial discourse, the answers that were given were silences. The participants were not literally silent, but were metaphorically silent. They did speak, but their speaking was an attentiveness to a different question, not the specific one offered by me to generate discussion. What resulted was a lengthy discussion about how the women in the group found themselves responding when faced with situations in which they had encounters with the Other, specifically a black male Other. The result is what I choose to term a veiled silence. Their whiteness was not articulated, but rather was conveyed only as a reaction to their encounter with the Other. The only way they did conceive of and therefore articulate their identity in a racial discourse was as a white female self in relation to a black male Other. The practice of answering their own question instead of the one that I had posed served as a veiled response that made their own whiteness invisible and unknowable, therefore inarticulable.

Perhaps these veiled silences reveal a whiteness not intelligible to these teachers, one beyond recognition of skin color. They experience themselves as white because they are not black, or any other "Other." When this occurs, whites do not see themselves as having a race except in opposition to another race. The absence of oneself as raced becomes apparent only when seen in opposition to someone else who is other. We are silent or utter a veiled response because we do not know how else to respond. Being raced is something that as whites we are rarely compelled to consider. As echoed by one of the participants, "Whites have always been sort of the non-race."

Intentional Silences. The youngest of the group members was a female in her mid-twenties who had revealed to me, but not to the group, that she was in a relationship with a black male. In the first group session, she alluded to this relationship but never spoke directly of it. Instead she spoke emotionally of the values and attitudes that she held which were entirely in conflict with those of her parents; however, she never directly stated that she was in a relationship with an African American man. She thus revealed her insecurities and fear of judgment through this declaration of an intentional silence.

In her case, the intentional silence speaks of her anticipation of how the group might respond in judgment of her embracement of the Other, something that by virtue of our whiteness she assumes us incapable of. Perhaps she questions whether or not the relationship is acceptable not just to others, but also to herself. She censors herself based on the context and what she perceives to be acceptable with this particular group of teachers, perhaps based on our silences or failures to acknowledge the relationship.

Unintelligible Silences. Do the spoken silences always mean something? I assert that they do, but I am not confident that their meaning is always discernible. Previously I mentioned the danger of echoing one's own fears and insecurities within the space of silence. It is for this reason that I make no attempt to understand every silence. Nor can I be so presumptuous as to claim that every silence is intentional, discernible, or knowable.

When I presented an initial draft of my interpretations of our conversations to the group, I was uncertain as to how they might respond. What might they hear themselves saying that they didn't recognize or wish to be made public? What if my desire to engage them as co-participants had also empowered them to censor me?

The reaction I got was peaceful, nonconfrontive, accepting, and affirming. What was being said in the absence of a reaction, in the silence of agreement? Because this was our last time to meet as a group, I can only suppose what these unintelligible silences might have been saying. Perhaps they were silences of agreement. Perhaps they stemmed from a failure to recognize racist attitudes. Perhaps they were silences of bewilderment in the face of the contradictions and inconsistencies found in some of their statements. What I know is that within these silences exist the traces that continue to reveal.

Silent Lessons

I have a kitten that entreats with a silent scream. She doesn't voice her desire, but the stretched jaws, the protruding tongue, the pleading eyes, the groping paws are far more imploring than if she were to mew like a "normal" kitten. I watch and listen to her more attentively than if she had an audible voice.

My intent is not to provide a prescriptive formula for how to listen to silence, nor a definitive categorization of all types of silences, but rather an argument for why listening to silences in discourse-based research can be both purposeful and meaningful. I have learned that attentiveness to empirical materials means different things. I have learned that the casting off of a traditional understanding of what counts as empirical materials worthy of consideration permitted me to hear beyond the traditional boundaries.

One of the important requirements of listening to the silence is to be aware of the possible inhabitants of the silence. Then one can probe the silences for the latent meanings and understandings found therein. A real danger in this methodological approach is our forcing the silences to say what we want to hear. It is essential that we listen for the meanings that are present (and absent) and the motivations and sources of those meanings—that we let the silence speak.

Had I been more attentive initially to the import of silence, I would, in my follow-up have had conversations with the participants, asking questions not only about what was being said, but what was being left unsaid. I would have explored further how they conceptualized race as part of their own cultural identity or heritage, plumbed more deeply how their awareness, or lack of awareness, of themselves as "raced" informed their encounter with the "Other," and I would have engaged them more fully in their response, or lack of response to specific questions, especially those they avoided or deflected by addressing an alternative question of their own creation. In the next chapter, I take up the question of how the interview is changed given an attention to these silences in the process of conducting interviews as I seek the silent lessons to be found in the excesses.

CHAPTER 7

Interviewing Within a Problematic of Silence

> I want to cultivate a method of patient listening, a reflex-
> ive method of looking, hearing, and asking that is dia-
> logic and respectful.
>
> —Denzin, 2002, p. 845

A Patient Listening

In the previous chapter I presented a process for listening to the silences in an analysis of discourse-based data. I described how, in the process of conducting the interviews, I had duti-fully crafted follow-up questions based on what the research participants were saying. What I had ignored, or rather failed to consider, was an opening up of the dialogue, not based on what the participants were *audibly* voicing but what they were *silently* voicing. This deafness to the silences present in the in-terview transcripts resulted in a failure to recognize how those silences had in fact shaped and limited the scope of the inter-viewer/interviewee exchange. While I may have come closer to cultivating a method of patient (silent) listening, I had failed to cultivate a method of inquiry in response to this listening.[1]

What were the filters that were censoring the silences *spo-ken* by my participants? Why was I unable to cultivate a method of inquiry in response to this silent listening? A possi-ble understanding provided by Briggs (1986) is that "the re-ceived methodology acts as a hidden filter, blocking our ability to hear what 'they' are saying while allowing the comforting sound of our own preconceptions about language and life to be echoed in the data" (p. 125). I had, it would seem, easily slipped back into the comfort of my perceived meaning and the

identity of my participants as presented in the words spoken—
words that I could *hear*, subsequently masking the silent echoes. How disappointed the specters must have been in me—
failing to cavort among the silent spirits filling the text with
their living, breathing presence. Just as the teachers in my
study were unable to lift the veil of their whiteness, I too was
unable to still the muffling effect of my received methodology.

Alicia Youngblood Jackson (2003) writes of "working the
limits of voice in qualitative research" (p. 693). What is to become of the interview encounter if we are to acknowledge, even
insist upon, the presence of a silent voice? The question is not
whether there is a silent voice present in the interview encounter, but rather, how as a researcher one might responsibly and
ethically engage this silent voice in the doing of the interview
without echoing one's own voice in the silent data, to work the
limits of voice in order to hear the voices silenced, not to fill the
silences with yet another voice of our own creation.

A glimpse of how we might begin to consider the practice of
actively engaging the silences in the doing of an interview is
provided by Laurel Richardson (1997) when she presents in the
form of field notes an ethnographic presentation that includes
her usually silent (at least to an observer) "interior monologue"
(p. 158).[2] This interior monologue is what she says to herself
(at the time) and records as part of her field notes and subsequent ethnographic presentation, but keeps silent or absent
from the dialogue that is occurring. These silences, her silences, inform her analysis, and perhaps her speech, but they
are kept from the hearing (at least initially) of those with whom
she is in dialogue.

To return to the notion of play so playfully engaged in
Chapter Three is to question/consider how the dynamic of an
interview encounter and the subsequent text that might be
elicited rather than missed might be reframed, reshaped, re-
imagined, if as researchers, we are to begin to seriously (but
with a playful approach) bring the silences to bear on this en-
terprise. By that I mean, what if we are to consciously (as
much as possible) frame the questions that we ask our participants—the questions that we withhold, the audible responses
that we garner, the silences overlooked—as essential aspects of
the dialogue that radically affect the outcome of our interviews,

whether we like to acknowledge them or not. What if we dare to meet the specter on the rampart at the stroke of midnight, not to contain the specter, nor to prove the specter's existence, but in a search for the ghostly intensity of language that we often miss so softly spoken in the mist. What if we are to engage in a dialogue with this specter, voicing questions that we fear, listening to the haunting replies, and evoking the silent monologue of ourselves and of our participants? What if we are to no longer contain our silent internal monologues but use them as the basis for our interactions with and questioning of our participants in our field sites?

Such a move, putting these silently articulated questions into play, requires an incisive awareness that not only permits a listening that has been impossible, but further demands an attentiveness and openness that has been absent. It demands of the researcher a removal of the white noise that serves to deaden and obscure the extraneous sounds.[3] To engage a problematic of silence in the doing of interviews is to begin the process of *listening to ourselves listening* with renewed vigor in order that we might be attentive to our own silenced/silent interior monologues and those of our research participants. For example, in the previous chapter, I included an entry from my research journal that expressed my hesitation and even fear at hearing myself, listening to myself as one being researched, and wondering what I might let slip in the silences that were heretofore unknown and unheard by me. Like Cixous (2001/1998), I had found peace in not seeing myself.

This process then of beginning to practice a silent reflexivity encourages a rethinking of the interview process, not as a further delimiting exercise that engages the notion of when an interview begins and ends, nor when data begins and ends, but a recognition that the interview is always happening as we consider those questions to ask and those that we consider too sensitive to ask, as we listen to what participants are saying and at the same time pay attention to what might be silently voiced, when we focus on what is said and what is not said as we construct follow-up questions and simultaneously begin the process of analyzing what is readily present and what is absently present. This act of incisive listening becomes alive in the field of play when we give up on the spoken word as a guarantor that "we know what we mean, mean what we say, say what we mean, and know what we have said" (Johnson, 1981, p. viii).

This silent interview methodology circles back on itself in much the same way as a "double science" as described by Patti Lather (1995),[4] producing discourses and practices that wander outside traditional ways of interviewing and knowing. This feminist deconstructivist methodology is not concerned with probing for more detailed responses nor is it a probing of respondents for more questions, both of which imply a penetration and linear mining of information. Rather, this methodology examines the layered messy construction of the writing of the text by researcher and researched through an interviewing process that includes the scraps of narrative and seeming diversions as well as those chosen specifically to assemble the narrative and stories presented. It is a process that relies upon these silent scraps not as mere filler, but as essential to the notion of speech that I have proposed which is both silent *and* spoken, both audible *and* inaudible, both given *and* withheld, both absent *and* present.

Spivak (1976) writes, "Fiction begins in the truth of the author and ends in the uncovering of that truth by the critic" (p. lxxiv). What then might be the truths that are being lived out in the "fiction" of rhetoric (to which we usually attend)? Are these truths primary or secondary to what is being said in the absences by our research participants? What then might we hope to uncover by listening to the absences—the scraps of conversation often skipped over and discarded in the digressions, pauses, and silences? Why should we begin to formulate questions both as a rejoinder to the voiced responses and to those responses that are silently voiced? These layered questions indicate a double practice of interviewing that does not differentiate between the so-called primary (spoken) and secondary (silent) text, but rather considers what is spoken in both the words providing structure to the text and the silences inhabiting their interstices.[5] This double practice means that the interviewer attempts to *listen* to the scraps of speech and the carefully crafted design of the pattern of speech and elicits an explanation of both. It seeks a messy, lumpy, ugly, and puckered text that can only begin to be complete in its inclusion of the incomplete, the unsaid, perhaps even the unthought.

Therefore, in order to develop strategies for interviewing within this problematic of silence, we must envisage these spoken silences as welcome visitors, as friendly ghosts if you will. The ghosts of cartoons and film provide a useful analogy— these ghosts can be seen as they pass over, around, behind, and between those "real" objects that we recognize, while at the same time (or sometime) are also invisible and undetectable. Just as the person in the cartoon or movie is often "tricked" by the wandering ghost into believing that the ghost is only present when seen, we know that even when the ghost chooses to hide, it is still present over, around, and behind what we consider to be "real." Thus, if we fall for the adage that seeing is believing, then we might also fall for the common wisdom that hearing is believing and fail to engage these silent ghosts ever present, and yes, frolicking, in the dialogue. We will then fail to move from a mechanized approach to interviewing that is obsessed with words spoken, toward a methodology that is equally obsessed with the words spoken between words.

"Crafting" a Silent Interview Methodology[6]

> Logic rules discourse, thought rules silence. (Heidegger, 1962a, p. 209)

The tools of the qualitative researcher are many, and while there are varied epistemological positions informing the deployment and limitations of said tools, the interview as a tool is widely accepted as an indispensable and taken-for-granted method for data collection (Mishler, 1986, p. 23). As Fontana and Frey (2000) suggest, "The interview and the norms surrounding the enactment of the respondent and researcher roles have evolved to the point where they are institutionalized and no longer require extensive training; rules and roles are known and shared" (p. 647). Perhaps because the interview is seen as commonplace, and because people encounter interviews in a multitude of settings and roles—job interviews, public opinion polls, credit checks, political forums, etc.—the attitude by many is that preparing for and conducting an interview involves no more than formulating a set of objectives, a corresponding "list" of questions that will enable one to achieve one's objectives, a comfortable, quiet, and confidential setting, and a means by which to record the answers "given" by the respondent.

Such a view, while commonplace, indicates a hierarchal, "call and response" exchange between the interviewer and interviewee, an enactment of reasoned questions and logical responses. This methodology often seeks to contain indeterminacies rather than one that functions to "explore and mobilize them as far as possible" (Stronach etal., forthcoming), or that allows for thoughtful, even silent, responses. Even within a feminist framework for interviewing that is collaborative and self-disclosing, what can often result is "What seems to be a conversation is really a one-way pseudoconversation" (Fontana & Frey, 2000, p. 658).

In response to an emphasis on methods of interviewing, Steinar Kvale (2006) has presented a view of "interviewing as craft." It is this idea of interviewing as craft that I am fostering in proposing methodological strategies that are intentionally creating a spacing and snagging of the narrative in order to allow the previously unheard, unthought, inaudible voices to be present, and to provide the basis for the questions formulated and asked.[7] This craft that I envision is a practice whereby the interviewer can reflexively train her or himself to notice and seek silent diversions and ask questions not just in response to what is audibly voiced, but to engage those specters threading themselves through the dialogue. This craft will also create practices of strategic surprise that enable the silences to be known to both the respondent and the interviewer and to elicit unpredictable responses, for as Derrida suggests, "To be worthy of this name, must a *response* not *surprise* us by some irruptive novelty?" (p. 347).

It is here that a slight diversion in the form of a caveat is warranted as I am beckoned by the silent specter frolicking about and disturbing my "rational" response. This specter with the bemused smile of a gargoyle is wondering if I am not "silently" advocating in this so called "craft" a glorified psychotherapy session. And to this specter I respond emphatically no!

I am not advocating that interviewers become psychotherapists, or even suggesting that qualitative researchers behave in a way that mimic the practice of psychotherapy (which opens up an entirely different set of ethical questions). However, there are practices and cues within many disciplines, including psychotherapy, that can teach qualitative researchers much about the "art" of questioning and the "craft" of creating a productive tension that encourages a thoughtful response. These insights gained from others can only aid us in being more attentive and responsive to the silent meanings of speech (both *in* words and *between* words), the specters glimpsed, and the boundaries transgressed.

Kvale (1996) wrote that the postmodern approach to interviewing "emphasizes the narratives constructed by the interview" (p. 38). The strategies that I propose are intended to focus on the narratives constructed in the context of the interview, but also aim to purposefully elicit those silent narratives inhabiting the shadows that we fail to notice. The craft of eliciting these silent narratives means that as researchers, we must listen for, listen to, and ask questions not just in response to an answer voiced, but to ask questions when we think a participant is withholding a response, or is giving a nonresponse, or is masking a response with words.

For example, in the same way that an interviewer uses a pause or a gap to allow a respondent time to reflect on her or his answer, the interviewer might also use a question to create a productive opening that will allow the silence to be given voice. Consider the following response by one of the teachers in my study as she described herself as being different from other members of her family and friends, and how an acknowledgment and questioning of the silence on my part might have led to a much more nuanced response on her part and subsequent understanding on mine. In the following I have, in the brackets, inserted the questions I might have asked in response to Anne's assertions, both silent and spoken.

Anne   I never really saw myself as prejudiced, but then I never really had to deal with any "other people." [Other people? Who do
            you mean by Other people?] So I was raised this way and
            now I've come to a *very, very*, very liberal, *very* open-minded
            understanding as far as my friends. [When you say liberal,

liberal, you mean...?] I'm also a single mother, as far as people who I go out on dates with, political views, everything and it's very, *very* conflicting with my parents. [How is that conflict lived out in your relationship with them?]

Not really, like my sisters with my generation, but its very hard for me because I'm confused a lot of the time, I'm torn. [Confused and torn, that sounds like another conflict. Why are you torn?]

You know, I want to do things with the person that I'm going out with right now and its wrong [How is it wrong? Why do you say that?] and I'm thinking, you know what's the difference if I get along with somebody or if my friend is Hispanic, or you know, [We don't know. What do you want us to know? Tell us what you mean?] what's the big deal....So I'm just real torn and my whole paper was just about how torn I am and how now that I'm, you know, [Again, what do you want me to know?] I'm thinking how you always find out who you are and sometimes I think that my family must look at me and say, "How in the world? Where did she come from and why is she like this? How could that happen?" [Boy, you just said a lot. Can you be more specific about how your values are in conflict with theirs?]

In this exchange with Anne, she leaves unsaid what she assumes I know, or perhaps what she hopes I do not know, or maybe have forgotten. What if I were to have asked at the time "What are you not saying?" or "Who are you not naming?" or sounding even more like a therapist in response to a long pause or gap in the conversation, "Why the pause?" or "What is the pause saying?" What if I would have been practiced enough and confident enough in myself as a skilled practitioner or "craftsperson" (Kvale, 2006) to have asked the silent questions that I have since inserted in the brackets or even to have been more pointed in the response? The questions may not have elicited a spoken clarification, they may not have resulted in a "desired" response, or Anne might simply have adroitly avoided the incisive opening. Even so, what may result in such a moment or moments is the creation of a productive tension, an opening for the participant to momentarily reflect on what she is not saying, or to identify (whether for herself or for me) what she is not saying. What may result is a spacing or interplay of conflicting views both audibly and inaudibly expressed. What may result is that the silences and denials are at the very least given a living presence. In the context of a group interview, it may also prompt the other participants to consider their own silences and what they may be revealing and withholding in these silences. These internal conflicts, the group knowledge that lives without words, even the complicities of phrases such as "you know" are now in the field of play and ready to be "heard."

For instance, I knew at the time of the group interview that Anne was in a relationship with a black man. As presented in the excerpt from the first group session, she alluded to her relationship without speaking directly to it. She spoke emotionally of the values and actions that she holds which are in conflict with those of her parents; however, she never came out and directly said that she was in a relationship with an African American man. What is she saying by her silence? Did she fear how we might respond to her because of her projected attitudes regarding Others vs. whites? Is she unsure herself if the relationship is acceptable (not only to others but also to herself)? Does she censor herself based on the context and what she perceives to be acceptable in a given situation or with a particular group of people? As researcher, I must consider not just her motivation regarding her behavior but also why I remained silent and did not try to get her to be more forthcoming. Was I hiding behind the veil of a nonthreatening "safe" feminist methodology? Perhaps the censors in my interior monologue were serving to gag the specters as effectively as Anne's were hers.

A further question that this re-listening and re-questioning of Anne exposes is a consideration of the possible markers of silence that may provide cues for interviewers of the silences yet to be questioned.[8] When Anne says, "you know," is the assumption that we in fact do know? Has "you know" become a commonplace way of saying something without articulating it, or do we ignore this marker as a substitute for a pause or moment of gathering our thoughts. For the speaker to decide that you in fact do know, so as not to have to state the obvious, or that I don't want you to know so I assume/pretend/convince myself that you know what is meant, or that I don't really know how to say what I mean so I conceal my "real" feelings with this seemingly innocuous statement is the implicit/explicit content of silence. Here is the conspiracy of silence, an agreed upon limit to conversation. To break this silence invites an aporia through which all manner of things might emerge. By attending to these and other such markers (you know, I mean, like, whatever) we, like those playful specters, find roguish and subversive means by which we invite and revel in the surprises bounding in and through the narrative. We orient ourselves as artful and craftful interviewers to receive these placeholders not as diversions, excuses, or an instance when the participant is at a loss for words, but to receive them in the same way that Hamlet receives the flourish of trumpets that announce the arrival of the Ghost of his murdered father. We shake ourselves out of a complacent listening (and questioning) that focuses solely on the words spoken as being that place where meaning resides and seek the meaning full absence of the present silence.

In Chapter Six, the silences were characterized as being meaning full, not necessarily intelligible, but meaning full nonetheless. By recognizing the silences that occur in the process of interviewing, we can openly address their presence, allow them to cavort with one another, and perhaps speak when they/we are ready. If, like the specter in Hamlet's tale, the specters in our research settings wish to be given a hearing, we will, by acknowledging their existence, by "listening," be able to "hear" the questions and content of their message. These silent voices, although playful and elusive, are real, not imagined, and require a different listening and openness to their absent presence.

While what I am advocating is an effective attentiveness to these silences, both in the process of conducting interviews and in making meaning of the transcripts and conversations, I want to reiterate the caution that in this methodological approach we must be leery of forcing the silences to say what we want them to say so that we hear what we want to hear. It is essential that we listen for the meanings that are present (and absent) and the motivations and sources of those meanings, that we let the silences speak to us and resist the temptation to fill those silences with our own voice. To do this is simply to add another layer to the rules that are "known and shared," or to risk the fate of a "failed" interview.

"Failed" Interviews[9]

Sometimes our participants may not want to be heard. I have had students in classes come to me in private and state that they don't speak in class because they fear ridicule, being seen as impolite, or worse, stupid. This practice of not speaking is sometimes further amplified in situations where the discussions center on issues of gender, race, or extremism and the students thereby risk revealing an "unacceptable" attitude. Perhaps these fears and concerns are also shared by participants in research situations and/or they may be disinterested, embarrassed, or don't trust us as researchers to treat their feelings and fears with respect and without condemnation. Maybe they choose to "keep their own counsel" resulting in a purposeful silence that if ignored on our part allows the interviewees to "win" the struggle of deciding what gets included and what gets left out. This is not to suggest that interviewing should be regarded as a contentious event but rather to further expose the etiology of the silences we encounter and the importance of being present to them.

Commensurately, if our research participants don't respond directly to our questions, or mask their silent words with trivial speech, or intentionally paint a picture which is contrary to their perception, i.e., skew the results, have we then "failed" in our attempt to conduct a successful interview? Qualitative methodologists have considered and written about what counts as interview data, what constitutes an interview, and when an interview begins and ends. Is not an equally important consideration that of what constitutes a "successful" interview? Is it only a success if our participants talk a lot and give us many words to code, categorize, and analyze? What of the words that they don't speak, or at least of the words that they don't speak in a conventional sense? While the questions accumulate in endless layers, they are nonetheless essential to the attentive awareness being considered in the interview process.

Karen Nairn and colleagues (2005) took serious note of these questions and wrote of their experience in conducting what they originally considered a "failed" interview because it failed to produce fat data and thick description. What emerged in their writing of a counter-narrative was a reimagining of what constitutes a successful interview and a return to the question of what counts as data. Despite the fact that the students in the failed interview did not feel safe and were not forthcoming with their responses, in fact were at times literally silent, the researchers reported that "we did hear things worth hearing, even during the early, more halting parts of the interview....The pauses, silences, inaudible comments, laughter and the audible text itself are all rich in meaning and convey how students feel unsafe as a result of not being able to understand their teachers, or for that matter their researchers" (p. 230).

Nairn (2005) and her colleagues learned that with the notion of interviewing that gave preference to words spoken, it was important to "not 'write-off' data that initially does not appear to be useful" (p. 239), in other words, the pauses, silences, and inaudible comments had much to say. As researchers engaging in this practice of craft, it is important to be attentive to the fact that what counts is not just the ways in which we view the interview, or the ways in which we wish to engage participants according to feminist and poststructural sensibilities, but of equal importance is knowing that those we are interviewing have probably experienced many examples of "one-way barrages of questions" (Fontana & Frey, 2000) where silence and pauses are not encouraged nor welcomed by the cues provided by the interviewer.

With this insight available, any charge that presents participants with the admonition to speak and thus break the silence must also take into account that when we are seeking to explore taboo subjects such as race, privilege, and sexual orientation, these teachers and students whom we wish to engage must first "unlearn to not speak" (Piercy, 1991). When silence is utilized as a means of "fitting in," remaining invisible, protecting the vulnerability to emotional/intellectual exposure, or simply avoiding calling attention to oneself (Ellsworth, 1997), it is important to realize that this silence may not always be intentional or devious but rather reflect a broader cultural insistence. The task then as researchers is to allow these digressions and pauses, uncomfortable and seemingly unproductive, to exist and bring into being a patient, active listening on our part.

Had I been more attentive initially to the import of silence, I would in my follow-up have had conversations with the participants inquiring not only of what was being said, but what was being left unsaid. I would have explored further how they conceptualized race as part of their own cultural identity or heritage, plumbed more completely how their awareness, or lack of awareness, of themselves as "raced" informed their encounter with the "Other," and I would have engaged them more fully in their response, or lack of response to specific questions, especially those they avoided or deflected by addressing an alternative question of their own creation. I would have indulged, even welcomed, the digressions, silences and resistances as detours to the as yet unintelligible truth, and recognized that once off the beaten path there was a new and exciting landscape emerging.

Digressions

> On the surface, there was always an impeccably realistic world, but underneath, behind the backdrop's cracked canvas, lurked something different, something mysterious or abstract.

> After pausing for a moment, she added, "On the surface, an intelligible lie; underneath, the unintelligible truth." (Kundera, 1984, p. 63)

Part of allowing the silences to speak and attending to those silences in our interviews with participants is developing a patience for digression, a casting aside of one's own agenda and timelines, a patient seeking out and listening for the unintelligible truths masked by the intelligible words. Shulamit Reinharz (1992) writes about feminist interview research as inviting and encouraging digressions. She described Susan Yeandle's approach to interviewing British women that purposefully built in this process of digressions, urging the women to tell their stories in their own way without the restrictions of rigid questions. "Women were always...encouraged to 'digress' into details of their personal histories (Yeandle quoted in Reinharz, 1992, p. 25). Reinharz continued by stating that "Clearly, Susan Yeandle valued the 'digression' as much as the core information and allowed interviewees to define the end of the story." In our zest for information and for getting the task completed, do we "fail" by not encouraging these digressions? If we view them as presenting extraneous or nonrelevant information, do we then quell the voice in the silence or, worse, ignore it, discounting its digressive richness? To do so is to continue to give preference to the "core" information clearly articulated and to relegate the "digressions" to a lesser status, or no status at all.

If, as feminist researchers or those engaged in social justice research we embrace participatory research in practice, then we must in our faithfulness to this methodology let go of our rigid agendas. This practice, by its very nature, calls us to fully engage the process and practice of digression which, in addition to allowing and encouraging our participants to shape the interview and its process, also allows and encourages the silent specters to create their own diversions in the fissures inhabited by their whispers. A silent interview methodology must not just allow for the digressions, but like Yeandle, must value and promote an opening and a forum for the digression, for it is in the process of digressing that silences are given freedom to speak.

Just as Fontana and Frey (2000) advise researchers in the field to "write everything down, no matter how unimportant it may seem at the time" (p. 368), interviewers must attempt practices that promote an attentiveness to the spoken *and* silent narratives, even those that seem irrelevant or extraneous. The quest is not to make judgments on the value of the silences or digressions, but to consider them as speaking and of providing a fertile ground for follow-up questioning. This requires a practice that does not preference audible speech or speech that directly answers or responds to a question posed by the researcher as an exclusive source of meaning, but also as a constraint to an openness to the meanings present in the digressions.

For example, in one of my research group's conversations we explored how teachers take their values into the classrooms including their perceptions of what is considered "normal" behavior in the classroom. During this discussion and following her earlier comment about how as teachers we are expected to excuse "certain behavior," (i.e., behavior that is not normal according to white middle class standards but that is exhibited by those Other students [another example of the silences speaking]), Marcy starts describing her experience attending the movie *Waiting to Exhale*. The following is an excerpt from her diversionary tale:

Marcy   I saw *Waiting to Exhale* with two girlfriends, both white, and they said to me the audience was the rudest bunch. I just want to say what they [her friends] said. They brought their babies, they commented, they said, "Yeah, go girlfriend." And we don't do that in the movie theater. They said that they ruined the movie for them. They asked if it bothered me and I said I just block it out, I'm used to it. I just block, and they weren't....They both work in a high class, white office, they're not used to that and they were shocked. I said, this is how it is.

I was sitting next to a black woman, she was saying, "Yo, all right!" to me and I didn't know her. I was annoyed by her. I listen to this all day. I didn't want to hear it on a Friday night.

I was thinking about that, it was like they took over the movie theater. They took control, like they owned it. I asked my psychologist what she thought, she's an upper middle class black woman, [as if she can speak for all black women] and she thought it was terrible, it portrayed the worst of their society, it was racist, but I kind of liked it.

And my kids saw it [the movie], and I hate to say race to them, they think I am prejudiced. And I asked them what it was like, and they said, well, it was a little noisier than usual, but they wouldn't say. And I asked them who was making the noise, kids? But I know who it was.

Lisa   I went to a play at CATCO [Contemporary American Theater Company] about two black women who get stranded in an office building in Atlanta on New Year's Eve. One is a cleaning woman and the other is one who has "made it" and the play is about their clash of cultures and the assumptions that they make about one another, and there were more blacks in the audience than there have been whenever I have been to a production at CATCO, because there are usually very few. And there was a lot of response by the blacks, but it felt to me like the blacks that were responding got the rest of the audience more engaged in what was going on.

Marcy   I did go to a play at the Jewish center and it was about Jewish people in Miami, and the audience members were talking and doing the same thing...but with the Jewish humor, they all were talking, so maybe it's just you identify with it.

Instead of my trying to teach or change Marcy's attitude by providing an example, how might the conversation have been changed if I had questioned the racist remarks contained in the silence as well as the apparent contradictions? If I had voiced my interior monologue that was later presented in the form of my analysis, and if I had focused on the digression as a strategic moment, rather than focusing on my critical, educative moment and a formulation of my next question, I believe the conversation would have taken a very interesting and informative detour. Instead I stayed on the main path (hid on it perhaps) knowing that I could ask those questions in the silent safety of my analysis. This, rather than attending to the silences and contradictions as they occurred, interrupting, even challenging the narrative, thus moving us off the path and into the fields where mud, thickets, grass, bogs, and messiness awaits instead of the predictable landscape of the well-manicured lawn.[10]

To accomplish this desirable detour is of course to reflexively train ourselves to invite and attend to these interruptions or awareness at the time they are occurring and to not worry about getting our new shoes muddy. If *Waiting to Exhale* had been a Jewish film and people were talking, would Marcy and her friends have experienced the same reaction? Or what if it had been a white audience reacting with comments or applause? Marcy had exhibited racist attitudes throughout the study, and she even knowingly named them at times, but I did no more to question/challenge the silent assumptions than did the others in the group. The ethical question of course is am I more responsible to challenge these unspoken and silently accepted racist attitudes as the researcher, interviewer, and group leader? Does a practice that unsettles the silences also lead to a further questioning of the silences? Are the diversions (both silent and spoken) more instructive than the so-called responses to our questions?

When Marcy stated, "I listen to this all day. I didn't want to hear it on a Friday night," what is implied in the absence that speaks volumes about the attitude she holds toward her black students? What is the intelligible lie masking the unintelligible truths of her attitudes toward her students? Where might this digression lead us? Further, when she remarks that she hates to say race to her children, is the assumption that if she doesn't name it, if she doesn't speak it, it doesn't exist? Is this palimpsest undetectable and therefore safely hidden until the researcher, attentive to the digressions and the silences, scratches just beneath the surface to let loose the meanings (specters) underneath?

A practice that unsettles these silences also depends on the digressions to challenge the limits of voice. The desire then is not to limit voice, both audible and inaudible, but to seek the limits of voice that contain the snags and interruptions, that are full of the irruptions of surprise and the ghosts behind the veils.

The Limits of Voice

> If, among all words, there is one inauthentic word, that word is certainly the word 'authentic.' (Blanchot cited in Stronach, 2002, p. 291)

We come now to the issue of desire in the purposeful pursuit of voice in discourse-based research. If, as Blanchot purports, there is no such thing as authenticity, then what is it that we desire and seek when we strive to record and represent participants' voices? If a desire for authenticity is no longer possible, then why the relentless pursuit of voice in qualitative research, particularly qualitative research that involves the practice of interviewing participants? Or perhaps, the more appropriate question is, what do we seek when we seek to give "voice" to our participants; what are we listening to/for in our effort to constitute voice?

An understanding of what counts as voice seems to limit those voices to which we attend in listening to our participants and devising follow-up questions. It also has implications for how we describe our participants' voices according to this understanding and inscribe their voices according to our own voices in our manipulation of data (Jackson, 2003, p. 697). Jackson continues in a discussion of the work of Michelle Fine and warns that in this process of description and inscription, we must pay attention not only to "*what* voices we hear" but also "*how* we hear them" in order that we not "idealize and totalize" (p. 697) their experiences as voiced and thereby ignore the messiness present. Furthermore, are we prone to leave out the silent voices in our narratives and, in so doing, deem them as unimportant or irrelevant digressions? I assert that in our zeal to gather data and make meaning, or to make easy sense, that we often seek that voice which we can easily name, categorize and respond to. A more fertile practice, however, would be to seek the voice that escapes our easy classification and that does not make easy sense.

If we only seek the voice of our participants that is easily discernible, easily understood, easily translatable, then what we seek is a normative language—one that is shared and designed for whoever must and can understand it (Derrida, 2001). We then limit such voice, or we fail to "work the limits of voice" (Jackson, 2003) satisfying ourselves with an interpretation, a translation that gets the job done but that ignores the silent voices, those that demand a "hard listening" (p. 698). In other words, we risk settling for a relevant translation.

> A relevant translation would therefore be, quite simply, a 'good' translation, a translation that does what one expects of it, in short, a version that performs its mission, honors its debt and does its job or its duty while inscribing in the receiving language the most relevant equivalent for an original, the language that is the most right, appropriate, pertinent, adequate, opportune, pointed, univocal, idiomatic, and so on. (Derrida, 2001, p. 177)

This quote begs the question, what do we seek when we "listen" to our participants? Is it the relevant translation that performs its mission by being readily discernible, knowable,

transparent? Or do we seek an irrelevant translation that performs its mission by being messy, opaque, polyphonic, and
nuanced—one that exceeds our knowing (easily) and understanding (quickly). Does our limiting of what counts as voice,
what we *hear* our participants saying and *how* we hear them
speaking serve only to smooth over that which is not knowable,
not discernible, and unpleasant?

When voice begins to exercise this excessive "messiness,"
we need to recognize how quickly we often move to contain it.
This desire to contain or to tame voice is so often couched in
the "right" translation that is appropriate and safe. Our "tam-
ing of the shrew," however, only circumscribes and delimits
those voices that threaten to entangle us in their web; it does
not "silence" them but we are left without their wise counsel.

I recently was the advisor for a student attempting to articulate her messy and contentious voice of which she had
quite a clear understanding and its potential to offend. This
voice was/is perceived as messy and contentious because it
was/is outside the normative ways of hearing and normative
ways of being in a small, Catholic, liberal arts college where an
overwhelming majority of the faculty are white. Here was a
young African American woman engaged in a qualitative research study being "heard" by an all-white committee consisting of (in addition to me, her education advisor), a
mathematician, psychologist, and chemist. Hers was a voice
that challenged the inequities in the treatment of African
American figures generally in her institution of higher learning,
but more specifically, in social studies textbooks. Her voice
pointed out that with the exception of a few, the only other
black faces that she saw among the staff were those who work
to cook and clean for the students and faculty.

The other members of the committee seemed concerned
with defining and limiting her voice in a way that "normalized"
her work. They commended her work as "important," and further characterized it as "creative," which translated as emotional rather than reasoned, biased and therefore
unprofessional. These members expressed serious reservations
about her work being a sound research project. I argued that
it represented not a "creative" narrative but a qualitative study,

not an emotional diatribe but a passionate account, not a "vit-riolic" exposé but a messy complicated text.

The committee finally approved the project, acquiescing, but not on the basis of its merit. They conceded because they were uncomfortable in having been implicated in the racist practices of the institution and, further, feared being accused as racist by the student. In their attempt to limit her voice, they also silenced their own.

The above example is rife with the ways in which we at-tempt to limit voice, what counts as worthy of being voiced (both substantive and methodological), and the fears associ-ated with voice that exceed the knowable limits. While discard-ing this student's (and mine for that matter) voice as irrelevant (e.g., outside the norm), one member of the committee went on to "commend [the committee members] for their desire to ex-periment with controversial topics and their general broad-mindedness, as well as their desire to give students a chance to express themselves and their opinions" (private e-mail corre-spondence addressed not to me, but to another member of the committee). The voices that they heard were not the conten-tious messy ones, but the safe and familiar ones. They were, as previously cautioned by Briggs (1986), deafened by their re-ceived methodologies which permit the affirming voices to be echoed in the din, but which contain and discard those un-comfortable ones.

This is the same trap awaiting us in the practice of inter-viewing. We can so earnestly latch onto these safe and familiar voices because they offer us rehearsed rebuttals, easy follow-up questions, and acute analysis. The question before us, however, is do we dare risk plunging into the abyss offered by the disruptive, uncomfortable, and sometimes, untranslatable voices?

A second thesis presented by another student to this same committee elicited a response on the part of one member as "quite simple to read and absorb." Clearly, this was not a messy qualitative text that was untranslatable, but rather, to return to Derrida, a "good" translation that performed its mis-sion. In order to resist this easy reading, this good translation, we must devise strategies for a troubled listening that summon the haunting specters in our midst and allow them to move our research in ever more searching directions.

A "Troubled" Listening

In describing the split text format for the book *Troubling the Angels*, Patti Lather (Lather & Smithies, 1997) explains that the "split text format puts the reader through a kind of 'reading workout,' a troubling exercise of reading" (p. 220). I consider interviewing within a problematic of silence and the art of listening to silence in the context of interviewing to require the same type of reading (listening) rigor needed to negotiate the levels and complexities of the text described. In the Lather and Smithies text, it is possible to read one narrative from beginning to end, and to ignore the interludes, sidebars, and parallel conversations. It is also possible to attend to all of them at once, and to choose which "text" is the primary one (at least for that moment).

In the same way, it is possible to listen to the words, to the "realist" tale (Van Maanen, 1988) being voiced by our participants without concern for the silent stories; however, in order to be faithful to a deconstructive methodology within a problematic of silence, it is imperative that we not give preference to the persistent and loud voice speaking to us. The methodological practice that Lather puts forth is one of a troubling exercise of reading that is necessary in a "reading" of the silent texts spoken in research encounters.

Writing in an early chapter of the above mentioned book, Lather and Smithies (1997) stated:

> Our hope is that each reader will work through the accumulating layers of information in the book and decide for themselves how it all comes together. Or more exactly, how the various layers of information about HIV/AIDS, researcher reflections and the women's stories interrupt one another into some place of not making any easy sense. At some level, the book is about getting lost across these various layers and registers, about not finding one's way into making a sense that maps easily onto our usual ways of making sense. (p. 52)

In the context of interviewing, I propose we seek a troubled listening that might help us get lost across the layers and registers of speech, both audible and inaudible, in order that we might trouble those silences long enough to shake them loose from their mooring, so that they, like us, will be lost and will speak to us in their attempts to get their bearings. By questioning these silences, troubling these listenings, we will relearn how to ask the questions previously silenced in our own interior monologues. Making "easy sense," while expedient and far less frustrating, puts us back in the same place that we were prior to this discussion. Making easy sense is what happens when we practice our received methodologies, silence the silence, ignore the irruptions and fail to test the limits of voice in qualitative research.

If we are not to make easy sense, then we are to attempt this rigorous reading, this troubled listening, this deconstructive practice that does not map easily onto our usual ways of making sense. It forces us to get lost in the narratives being performed so that we might approach our listening and our questioning of these performative texts with the same vigor and skepticism with which we approach a written text. It beckons us to be reminded to consider the competing tendencies in the data and to consider not just the dominating narratives but also those echoing in the muffled subtext. If we are simply to focus our listening on the spoken words, we might as well just engage interviewing via e-mail correspondence. We can pose questions to participants, they can record their responses, and we go on our way.

A troubled listening also means that we listen against the categories that we create as we listen to responses. We give up on trying to anticipate the direction of a response so we can formulate our next question, or to put the response into a category so we can place a checkmark in the appropriate box. A troubled listening goes beyond a reflexivity, although that is a prerequisite, toward an ongoing process of listening to ourselves and attempting to unmask the veils through which we filter what we say, what we ask, and what we hear. It means that we acknowledge the limits of language and attempt a listening and asking that confronts these limits. Such a listening requires courage and a willingness to break our own silences and to ask the questions that we dare not ask, that we prefer not to ask, that we prefer not to hear. It is by itself an enactment of a deconstructive methodology. It means as researchers that we give up on the possibility of the possible and seek the constant boundlessness of what our participants have to say. In other words, we actively try to get lost in the layers of the narrative in order to loosen ourselves from only listening to (or listening for) sounds.

In the context of interviewing, a troubled listening invites productive ways of not making easy sense. It requires the introduction of silent reflexivities whereby the interviewer can invoke practices of strategic surprise that call attention to the silences. It means that as qualitative researchers we seek practices that cause a listening that does not anticipate the expected response, but one that elicits an irruptive surprising response. It is a listening and asking that exceeds the questions and that seeks a silent transgressive discourse. It is a coming to silence that is intent upon working the limits of voice.

CHAPTER 8
Coming to Silence

Undisciplined Questions

> In the introduction to my *Search for a Perfect Language* (1995), I informed the reader that, bearing in mind the physical limits of a book, I had been forced to omit many curious episodes, and I concluded: "I console myself that I have the material for future excursions in erudition." (Eco, 1998, p. vii)

It is my hope, particularly if you have ventured this far into my tales of silence, that you not consider this text to be an excursion in erudition without purpose, but an excursion in coming to silence. When I first responded to this siren call of silence my outline indicated a prescriptive ending, a presentation of categories of silence that might help us, as researchers, *listen* to/for the silences that I had encountered in my work and to provide *tangible* examples of the silent specters inhabiting the site of my/our research. A rather *impossible* task and not what one would call a deconstructive move.

"Nietzsche has already pointed out that the ability of an idea to comfort us is no criterion of its truth" (Caputo, 1986, p. 253), and yet it was this comfort and truth that I was proposing (and perhaps secretly longing). Perhaps I had grown weary of the nagging presence of the specter and hoped that I might elude it for a moment as I retreated into the blithe comfort of my own silent cocoon, into the comfort of not seeing and not hearing myself, into the comfort of untroubled meaning. Possibly that and also a longing for acceptance, validation, and agreement that yes, what I was attempting was *real* (not some ghost of my own creation), that I was in fact engaging in empirical work (not just an echo of my own silenced voices), and that no, I had not given up on meaning (all past claims that have been made about this pursuit of mine). Rather, I had become obsessed with the excesses and breaches that inform our previously held (and limited I might add) notions of meaning and speech and while perhaps momentarily considering such a retreat, could no longer find solace in the peace of silences and specters ignored. So where does this leave me, or rather, having begun, whence now?

In my attempt to fulfill my promise, *Putting Poststructural Theory to Work,* I felt that the reader (and my publisher) might feel cheated if I were to not make good on my word, which you know if you have stayed with me this far, is not worth the paper it is printed on. Or put another way, it exceeds the type and the signs, already ontologically disciplined by signifiers such as data, research, speech, silence, and meaning (Stronach, 2002). Such a move then would result not in the uncontainable energy of speech as discourse, but the containable response of silence as knowable, or as Derrida would say, as translatable.

How then to come to the end (not last) page of this haunting tale, this search for specters, this impossible pursuit. It is to welcome the undisciplining performances of these signifiers possible only through a deconstructive methodology. It is to open up the possibility of a blank space,[1] not one that is empty, but one that is overflowing with the fullness of absence. And while this space of writing, of research, of writing about research is already disciplined, I seek an undisciplining,

an opening,

a tearing,

a snagging,

a spacing,

a troubling

that resists the overwriting

by the polarity of theory/practice, voice/silence, data/diversion, absence/presence, meaning/nonsense, interviewing/conversation, science/nonscience,

et cetera, et cetera, et cetera.

As a result of this writing, this listening, this snagging nagging presence of silence, questions continue to emerge that assure me that there is no end to this silent talk, to this talk of silence, this echoing and haunting absent presence. What remain are only undisciplined questions that welcome the voices of the specters. It is with the diversions and listenings that I place myself on the last page of this book and at the beginning of this task, for "If I have multiplied the detours and the contortions...it is because I am here, I am placed, I have placed myself, in an untenable position and before an impossible task" (Derrida, 2002, p. 353). I am before an impossible task that presents the possibility of continuing to listen to the previously unacknowledged and unheard silences. This untenable position finds me at the edge of the canyon listening to the unending echo of silent questions and silent leavings that warrant further consideration, further travels in erudition and further conversation. It places me at a thinking of the limits of knowing as I consider the limit of silence.

Thinking the Limit of Silence

> Deconstruction is seen as hyperconceptual...It therefore attempts to think the limit of the concept; it even endures the experience of this excess; it lovingly lets itself be exceeded. It is like an ecstasy of the concept: a *jouissance* of the concept to the point of overflowing. (Derrida & Roudinesco, 2004/2001, p. 5)

I use these undisciplined questions in my attempt to think the limit of silence to the point of overflowing in a way that expresses my project from the start—thinking silence not as absence but as presence, not as lack but as excess, as *meaning full* and *purpose full*. But first, in order to think this limit, to move beyond merely a theorizing of silence is to conceive of and speak of voice and speech, not as one element of the hierarchy of speech/silence to be dismantled or shaken up, but to move toward a conception of, thinking of, and *speaking that is at the same time speech and silence*. That *is* presence and absence.

But how do I in my talk of silence continue to limit the concept of silence by the very language and practice by which I attempt to name and translate? How can I resist a translation that gets the job done but that ignores the silent voices? How do I let the leave taking from the last page not result in some nice tidy "ending" that acts in such a way as to merely reinscribe that which I am trying to think the limit of? The very fact that the methodological project in which I am entangled causes me to still speak of speech as separate from, different than, distinguishable from silence is to continue to reinscribe the binary. In a working of the limits of data, speech, and silence, how might I continue toward a blurring of the boundaries, a spacing of the speech acts, a snagging of the narratives that illuminate our continuing attachment to meaning found in words? This again is not an attempt to say that meaning is not found in words, but if we are to rely solely on words or primarily on words, then we adhere to "a language game wherein what is said is a faithful narrative of what is lived and known" (Macbeth, 2001, p. 44) and we fail in what Macbeth (citing Lather) terms a "skepticism toward 'innocent' speech" (p. 48). I seek methodological practices that will *not* allow us to make meaning from the words without an inclusion of the silence in the gaps, that demand skepticism of innocence in words spoken, and toward practices that will impel us to consider the total phenomena as educational ethnographers in pursuit of the overflowing fullness of silence.

Thinking the limit of silence means that more work must be done to trouble the limits and assumptions that constrain the ways in which we encounter data, ask questions, and hear answers. One way to attempt this limit is to develop strategies in our struggle to make our own silences audible as researchers. It is to continue the discussion begun in Chapter Seven, to develop reflexivities of silence. Such practices seek to purposefully inject moments of strategic surprise

in order

that we might catch ourselves

and our participants

just off balance enough

that

the guard is

dropped

and the silences spilled.

In my continued research and in my attempts to enact these reflexivities of silence, encountering the practices as I enact them, I sense this is the place to make use of what Derrida (Derrida & Roudinesco, 2004/2001) refers to as an "insistent and explicit deconstruction," a deconstruction "meant to not be only theoretical or speculative but concrete, effective, political" (p. 23). To achieve such means that I redeem the promise, or at least the impossibility of the promise, of putting poststructural theory to work in qualitative research after all.

In the text *Counterpath* (Malabou & Derrida, 2004), Derrida enacts the performative stance of deconstruction through the postcard as a figure of a written text. Derrida writes cards back to Malabou that are inserted into the book, and by this act threatens the certainty of the text. The postcard is written and can be sent, or can be lost before it is sent, or can be forgotten, or if it is in fact mailed, it can get lost in the mail. The messages can/may be read by the intended reader, or by others along the way, and in fact they are in this instance read by both. The sender cannot guarantee, if the recipient receives the card, which side he or she will read. What will the recipient find more interesting about the card: the photograph, the postage stamp, the scribbled message that may or may not be decipherable? If the postcard does in fact arrive at its destination, it may be preceded by the sender who arrives before the mail is delivered. So if the card arrives, it can have new effects, unintended effects, or no effect if it is lost, or at least no discernible effect on the intended receiver. And how will the sender ever know if the card was received, or how it was received?

When a lover sends a postcard, does she or he include messages on the postcard that are encrypted in ways so that only the intended receiver can "know" what the "true" meaning is? What if the receiver incorrectly interprets these coded messages, these messages that appear in the words between words? What if these words are lost in translation? Are there words between words in the postcards that Derrida sends to Malabou that are missed by us? Do we make more of the words written than was ever intended by Derrida? What are the excesses that we inscribe as we make meaning of the words written and the words left unwritten, of the words between words?

So many unanswered/unanswerable? (impossible?) questions. But let us treat the speech acts enacted by participants in our research sites as postcards mailed to us and treat their words as messages that may or may not reach the intended receiver. Yes, this is to treat the words as sometimes secondary to the postage stamp, the photograph, the crypted message decipherable by the intended receiver, but with meanings conveyed and made by the unintended receiver as well.

This practice of enacting deconstruction through the writing of the text via postcards may be likened to the practice of enacting reflexivities of silence in the act of interviewing and data analysis. It is to enact practices that turn speech on itself in order to engage reflexivities of silence that mimic the sending of the postcard. It is to treat all of the elements of the metaphorical postcard (words spoken, gestures enacted, glances averted, nervous laughter instead of a response, avoidance of a topic, diversionary tales, "filler" masking as response) as having effects, both intended and unintended, all of which contribute to the delight and surprise of receiving an unexpected postcard, especially if received from our lover.

If we receive the postcards sent by our participants as having landed in our mailbox as a result of a circuitous and haphazard journey, then we may receive them not as conveyers of meaning or truth in the words written, but as undisciplining texts that interrupt

data,   speech   and

        meaning,

not in an effort to do away with meaning, but in an effort to maximize the freeplay of "speech acts." In other words, we allow ourselves to take off on a journey without a fixed destination. We give ourselves permission to get lost,[2] to go off *not* in a direction that is predictable or knowable,

but a direction certain to

intrigue,   provoke,   unsettle,

disturb,

and to open up a dialogue between speech and thought, between what is audibly voiced and what is silently stated. We embark on a deconstructive journeying that allows those uncharted silences to

speak,   breathe,   and

exceed   the   limits of   our

knowing

as we continue to pursue the undisciplining nature of

inhabited   silence

in qualitative research.

NOTES

Preface

1. Question posed by Dan Miller in the graduate course *Radical Theology* taught by John Caputo, Autumn 2005, Syracuse University.

2. In *The Mystical Element in Heidegger's Thought*, John Caputo (1986) discusses how "Heidegger wants to hear what is drowned out for the rest of us" (p. 67). He promotes a more careful listening in order to render hidden the depths previously unheard (p. 94). Where I differ in my pursuit of silence or of the nothing as something experienced or encountered is that I do not seek the presence of a primal language or language as being the boundary of Being. Neither do I pursue silence as a condition for authentic language (p. 224–225).

Chapter 1

1. During the fall semester 2005, I travelled to Syracuse University monthly and participated in two graduate courses taught by John D. Caputo. Upon arriving for the first class session, I was introduced to the students as being there to talk about silence—an impossible task! While I have tried to indicate quotes from my conversations and participation in classes, I am sure that there exists in my text the presence of Caputo's words and wisdom that I have been unable to separate from the voices of the specters that haunt and inform me.

2. I borrow this notion of "troubling" from Patti Lather, who discusses the notion of doing and troubling at the same time in order that as methodologists we work "at the edges of what is currently available in moving toward a science with more to answer to in terms of the complexities of language and the world" (1993, p. 673). Her work is grounded in an endless pursuit of "troubling," and for this I am forever grateful. She too is a haunting presence for me in this text.

3. A pertinent aspect of this research and one becoming increasingly critical is the demographics of the population of teachers compared to the population of students in U.S. schools. The *Digest of Education Statistics*, 2002, stated that in 1996, 90.7% of teachers in public schools were white, non-Hispanic, 7.3% were black, non-Hispanic, and 2% were classified as other (National Center for Education Statistics, 2000). Further, the National Center for Education Statistics (2000) reported that in the top 100 school districts, 66.9% of the student population is classified as minority. If you consider the top 500 districts, 56.7% of the students are classified as minority, and these percentages continue to increase. In a class I teach, "Diversity and the Learner," I ask my mostly white students at the beginning of each semester to develop a laundry list of characteristics with which to describe themselves to a stranger, and any reference to an ethnic or racial identity is generally not included, while they most often do include such distinctions when describing students of color with whom they work in schools. This is significant because they see only the mark or distinction related to race and ethnicity as someone "other" than they are, i.e., not white.

Chapter 2

1. The specters and the silences are always already present in our research encounters and in the conversations. Throughout this book, I rely heavily on the

ontological haunting in Jacques Derrida's *Specters of Marx* and Derrida's use of Shakespeare's Hamlet to illustrate this hauntological effect. Given my reading (or mis-reading) of Derrida, I am prompted to consider the following questions: What ghosts are haunting the data? How can I use the metaphor of the ghost to prevent the methodological structures from closing over, from preventing the possibility of the impossible? What are the multiplicity of voices and meanings conveyed by the specters?

Whether we choose to recognize the silences and the absences as presence are methodological and epistemological considerations. Ian Stronach (2002) writes, "This space is not yet blank" (p. 291). "Before we write or speak or read, the space, silence, and blank are already ontologically disciplined, disciplining, writing, written, speaking, spoken, "uncovering as we cover it" (p. 292). In other words, before we listen to our participants or analyze our transcripts, the silent specters are beckoning and speaking with a multiplicity of voices and meanings, speaking their story outside the limits of our attempts to contain them.

2. In the introduction to the 2nd edition of *The Handbook of Qualitative Research*, Norman Denzin and Yvonna Lincoln (2000) write of the "seven moments of qualitative research." They describe the sixth (postexperimental) and seventh (the future) as being upon us and as being characterized as a further challenging of previous epistemologies, some as yet to be named.

3. It is important to dispel the perception that I am not interested in a monitoring of the literal silences or of the social patterns that produce silences that would be of interest to ethnomethodologists. I am interested in considering the "marks" that our participants make in the process of speaking, the traces present in speech as the silent marks in air.

Chapter 3

1. In keeping with a deconstructive move that destabilizes and that unseats the resident hierarchies, my project examines the way in which we order speech and silence, giving preference to voiced speech as being the foreground of speech, that which is noticed, and silence as being the background of speech, that upon which voiced speech is located. This move then seeks to decenter the privileged position given to voiced speech, and listens to silence not as background, but also as foreground. It attempts to unmask the visual representation that allows another image to appear when our perceptual frame is interrupted. An example is the image that contains an urn or two profiles, depending on what the viewer sees as the figure (foreground) and what the viewer sees as the ground (background). Another example is the image in which the viewer either sees a beautiful young woman or an old woman.

2. I first introduced the idea of a poetic of silence in an article that appeared in the journal *Qualitative Inquiry* (Mazzei, 2003). Some of those ideas are presented in this section of Chapter Three, but I further extend a discussion of thinking about a problematic of silence in Chapter Four, and how a treatment of our conversations with participants as poetic constructions in Chapter Five opens up this space for life and meaning to breathe and speak as described by Kelly, Stern, and Hass.

3. For a further discussion, see Dunbar, Rodriguez, and Parker (2002), in which they discuss how race and subjectivity impact the interview process, and specifically discuss that the reason some respondents remain silent or inarticulate regarding race is not evidence that they have nothing to say, but is explainable through a consideration of other factors. (They specifically take up this discussion on pages 287-289.)

4. My thanks to Jack Caputo for this lovely description presented in an e-mail. He further discusses this idea in Chapter Five of the text, *The Mystical Element in Heidegger's Thought* (Caputo, 1986).

5. Like Heidegger, I seek that which is drowned out. "Like Eckhart, Heidegger too insists that the primal language can only be heard in silence. Too many words drown out what is being said (Caputo, 1986, p. 167). Unlike Heidegger, I do not seek silence as the perfect language, nor as a primal language. For a further discussion, I refer the reader again to the above referenced text.

Chapter 4

1. I engage in the play that occurs here between Derrida's idea of *play* and Richardson's (1997) book that contains the enactment of her interior monologue entitled *Fields of Play*.

2. In the book *Rogues*, originally published in France under the title *Voyous*, Derrida uses the term *"Etat voyou,"* the French equivalent of rogue state. In this text he challenges the ways in which the policy of global powers (most notably the U.S. and U.K.) label those countries as rogues that interfere with received notions of democracy and progress. It is this outlaw designation of rogue that I am evoking when I write of roguish data—that which is unforeseeable, unpredictable, and outside the normative boundaries.

Chapter 5

1. The image of the heartbeat of the poetic voice is inspired by the title of the book by Alfred Corn (1998), *The Poem's Heartbeat*. The book is an introduction to prosody—the art and science of metrical composition in poetry. While I have not quoted Corn directly, his

discussions of what is audible in poetry, the levels of stress in poetic form, how we are trained to hear language, and how we must train ourselves to listen, inform my understanding and description of a poetic of silence.

Chapter 6

1. My thanks to Bettie St. Pierre for this wonderful insight.

Chapter 7

1. Kvale (2006) and others have written about an acknowledgment of the interview encounter as constructed and manipulative no matter how much we attempt or claim the participatory and/or dialogic nature of the interview. This cautionary note is particularly important when one begins to listen to and evoke responses from participants based on their silent replies. It then becomes increasingly important to attend to those methodological practices that seek to open up the space for an honest (as much as possible) and meaningful dialogue through the establishment of rapport, prolonged engagement, and multiple interviews.

2. In an ethnographic presentation, "The Case of the Skipped Line," Richardson (1997) has created a script that is a representation of a panel and subsequent discussion at the 1990 Society for the Study of Symbolic Interaction Conference. In discussing the writing of this drama, she explains, "Once the drama was written, I cast members of my family into the roles and tape-recorded them....I left blank time on the tape for me to speak live what I had been thinking but did not say in 1990. I did the ethnographic performance at the 1992 SSSI meetings, using the prerecorded tape and speaking out loud in 1992 what was unspoken in 1990" (p. 157).

It is an attention to this interior monologue in the form of the questions that we don't ask, that we might ask, that we choose not to ask that I wish to evoke in the process of interviewing. This is not to be understood in terms of examining what I repress as an interviewer, but what I fail to ask because I am not asking questions of the entire conversation because I have failed to ask the questions as prompted by those remarks made in silence.

3. I refer here to the "white-noise" machines often found in the offices of physicians and therapists that serve to deaden and muffle voices in an effort to white out what is being said in the privacy of an examination room, or a therapists office, so that those in other rooms, outside the door, or passing down the hall are unable to hear the conversation.

4. This "double science" is one that "argues the need for a proliferation of eccentric kinds of science to address the question of practice in postfoundational discourse theory" (p. 64). Citing the work of Brantlinger and Ulin, Patti Lather (1995) presented the idea of "double practices, both science and antiscience, both obvious examples of disciplinary discourse of the human sciences and wanderers outside of the scientific paradigm" (p. 64). Their discussion of the genealogy of science, a probing of identities and interpretations, and the nomadology of science, the wanderings that transgress traditional boundaries of science, led her to the idea of a "double science."

5. Spivak (1976), writing about deconstruction, states, "The so-called secondary material [silence] is not a simple adjunct to the so-called primary text [what is spoken]. The latter inserts itself within the interstices of the former, filling holes that are always already there" (p. lxxiv). My insertion of silence and the spoken into the brackets is an enactment of deconstruction in the proc-

ess of both questioning the silences and acknowledging and interpreting the silences.

6. I refer here to the paper presented at the AERA Annual Meeting by Steiner Kvale (2006), "Interviewing Between Method and Craft," and that I take up later in this section.

7. In a conversation with Ian Stronach after he had reviewed a draft version of this chapter, he commented that I was still very attached to the ideas of spaces and gaps in a materialist sense, rather than the movement of deconstruction that I had tried to establish in earlier chapters—a movement of deconstruction that is an interplay of spacing, that is an open-ended spacing which serves to keep the future (and therefore the possibility of the impossible) endlessly open and that is not formalizable. In one of his lectures, Caputo stated that we cannot stop the flow of deconstruction, for if we do, we have fixed meaning and therefore have arrested the play, in other words, we have stopped thought. If Derrida is right about deconstruction, then Derrida does not have the final word on deconstruction.

Trying to shake myself loose from the need/desire to fix meaning, to find some stability amidst the unstable nature of this work, I returned to Derrida (1981/1972) and the image of the snag in language that he discusses in *Dissemination.* "Dissemination endlessly opens up a *snag* in writing that can no longer be mended, a spot where neither meaning, however plural, nor *any form of presence* can pin/pen down {*agrapher*} the trace" (p. 26). And so I am attempting to be mindfully aware of the silent specter of the mother tongue that attempts to remove the play of the trace, and to beckon the specter that is engaged in disrupting, snagging, and undoing the structures.

8. This idea of the grammatical markers of silence emerged from a conversation with Maggie MacLure in response to

an earlier draft. While I mention these markers and provide some possible examples in this section, there is much room to more fully explore these markers and their effects in the process of conducting interviews.

9. I refer here to the article by Nairn, Munro and Smith (2005), entitled "A Counter-narrative of a 'Failed' Interview."

10. The following is an entry from my research journal written at the time.

Journal entry, January 14, 1996:
Phillip and I went to see *Waiting to Exhale* this evening. Two observations that I made, probably instigated in response to Marcy's comments this afternoon. There were some white characters in the film, although they were in secondary or background roles. A major white character who we only "see" momentarily is the woman that Bernie's husband is having an affair with.

The other observation which may have otherwise gone unnoticed was a segment shown before the previews. It was a "don't talk during the film you may disturb your neighbors" reminder. I have seen this same message at this theater before; however, it is not a customary lead-in that they show before every film, in fact it is seldom used. I wish I could remember now the other films that they have used it with (other so-called black films?).

Journal entry, February 6, 1996:
I telephoned the Theater yesterday to follow-up on my supposition about their use of a "don't talk during the film" reminder shown before *Waiting to Exhale*. The woman that I spoke with confirmed the fact that they do not show it before most features, and that usually, but not always, it is a planned decision. As I started pressing her as to the critieria, she stated that it was based on the projected demographics the film was expected to draw. "For example, if it is an animated film expected to

draw college students, we will use it. And I don't want this to sound racist, but there are certain cultural groups who respond in different ways, some audiences tend to be more rowdy than others."

When I told her that specifically I was asking about its use before *Waiting to Exhale*, she confirmed that yes, it had been purposefully shown before screenings of the film. When I asked if this would be typical for "so-called black films" she also confirmed my supposition.

Chapter 8

1. Ian Stronach (2002) writes of the disciplining and over-writing that is present before we put pen to paper, or give voice to thoughts. "This space is not yet blank. Before I write, it is over-written by the polarity of theory/practice....It is a space that is spoken for, before any discipline speaks. It is an invisible writing already riting" (pp. 291-292). I seek this over-writing, not as a determinant of meaning, but in order to irrupt the so-called blank spaces in pursuit of the excesses of meaning, not that limit, but according to Stronach, that continue to write/rite new meanings.

2. In a lecture given on October 12, 2005, in a discussion of the Malabou and Derrida text, John Caputo began the lecture by stating, "If we were all more lost we would be better off." This practice of getting lost has also proven to be the source of productive theorizing for Patti Lather as evidenced by an earlier quote from the text *Troubling the Angels*, and her forthcoming book, *Getting Lost: Feminist Efforts Toward a Double(d) Science*.

BIBLIOGRAPHY

Asimov, E. (2006, April 19). Shh. It's time for the chablis to speak. *The New York Times*, p. D8.

Baker, P. (1995). *Deconstruction and the ethical turn*. Gainesville, FL: University Press of Florida.

Bhabha, H.K. (1994). *The location of culture*. London: Routledge.

Billig, M. (1997). Keeping the white queen in play. In M. Fine, L. Weis, L.C. Powell, & L. Mun Wong (Eds.), *Off white: Readings on race, power, and society* (pp. 149–157). New York: Routledge.

Bogdan, R.C. & Biklen, S.K. (1992). *Qualitative research for education: An introduction to theory and methods* (2nd ed.). Boston: Allyn and Bacon.

Briggs, C.L. (1986). *Learning how to ask: A sociolinguistic appraisal of the role of the interview in social science research*. New York: Cambridge University Press.

Britzman, D. (2000). "The question of belief": Writing poststructural ethnography. In E.A. St. Pierre & W.S. Pillow (Eds.), *Working the ruins: Feminist poststructural theory and methods in education* (pp. 27–40). New York: Routledge.

Brook, C.J. (2002). *The expression of the inexpressible in Eugenio Montale's poetry: Metaphor, negation, and silence*. Oxford: Oxford University Press.

Buechner, F. (1977). *Telling the truth: The gospel as tragedy, comedy, and fairy tale*. San Francisco: Harper & Row, Publishers.

Caputo, J.D. (1997). *The prayers and tears of Jacques Derrida: Religion without religion*. Bloomington, IN: Indiana University Press.

———. (1993). *Against ethics: Contributions to a poetics of obligation with constant reference to deconstruction*. Bloomington, IN: Indiana University Press.

———. (1978). *The mystical element in Heidegger's thought*. New York: Fordham University Press.

Carrol, L. (1999). *Alice in wonderland*. New York: North-South Books. (Original work published 1866).

Cixous, H. (2001). Savoir. In H. Cixous & J. Derrida, *Veils* (Geoffrey Bennington, Trans). Stanford, CA: Stanford University Press. (Original work published 1998).

———. (1993). *Three steps on the ladder of writing* (S. Cornell and S. Sellers, Trans.). New York: Columbia University Press.

Cixous, H. & Calle-Gruber, M. (1997). *Rootprints: Memory and life writing* (E. Prenowitz, Trans.). London: Routledge. (Original work published 1994).

Clair, R.P. (1998). *Organizing silence: A world of possibilities.* Albany, NY: SUNY Press.

Constas, M.A. (1998). The changing nature of educational research and a critique of postmodernism. *Educational Researcher, 27* (2), 26–33.

Cook, J.J. (1964). Silence in Psychotherapy. *Journal of Counseling Psychology, 11*(1), 42–46.

Corn, A. (1998). *The poem's heartbeat: A manual of prosody.* Ashland, OR: Storyline Press.

Danow, D.K. (1997). *Models of narrative: Theory and practice.* New York: St. Martin's Press.

Dauenhauer, B.P. (1980). *Silence: The phenomenon and its ontological significance.* Bloomington, IN: Indiana University Press.

Denzin, N.K. (2002). The cinematic society and the reflexive interview. In J.F. Gubrium & J.A. Holstein (Eds.), *Handbook of interview research* (pp. 833–847). Thousand Oaks, CA: Sage Publications.

Denzin, N.K. & Lincoln, Y.S. (2000). Introduction: The Discipline and Practice of Qualitative Research. In N.K. Denzin & Y.S. Lincoln (Eds.), *Handbook of qualitative research* (2nd ed., pp. 1-28). Thousand Oaks, CA: Sage Publications.

Derrida, J. (2005). *Rogues: Two essays on reason* (P.-A. Brault & M. Naas, Trans., W. Hamacher, Ed.). Stanford, CA: Stanford University Press. (Original work published 2003).

———. (2002). *Negotiations: Interventions and interviews 1971–2001* (E. Rottenberg, Trans., Ed.). Stanford, CA: Stanford University Press.

———. (2001). What is a "Relevant" Translation? *Critical Inquiry, 27*(2), 174–200.

———. (2000). *Of hospitality: Anne Dufourmantelle invites Jacques Derrida to respond* (R. Bowlby, Trans.). Stanford, CA: Stanford University Press. (Original work published 1997).

———. (1994). *Specters of Marx: The state of the debt, the work of mourning, & the new international* (P. Kamuf, Trans.). New York: Routledge. (Original work published 1993).

———. (1992). Passions: 'An oblique offering' (D. Wood, Trans.). In David Wood (Ed.), *Derrida: A critical reader* (pp. 5–35). Oxford, UK: Blackwell.

———. (1991). Letter to a Japanese friend. *A Derrida reader: Between the blinds.* (pp. 270–276). P. Kamuf (Ed.). London: Harvester.

———. (1982). Différance. In *Margins of Philosophy* (A. Bass, Trans.). Chicago: The University of Chicago Press. (Original work published 1972).

———. (1981). *Dissemination* (B. Johnson, Trans.). London: The Athlone Press. (Original work published 1972).

———. (1978). Structure, sign and play in the discourse of the human sciences. In *Writing and difference* (A. Bass, Trans.). Chicago: The University of Chicago Press. (Original work published 1968).

———. (1976). *Of grammatology* (G. C. Spivak, Trans.). Baltimore: The Johns Hopkins University Press. (Original work published 1967).

Derrida, J. & Caputo, J.D. (1997). *Deconstruction in a nutshell: A conversation with Jacques Derrida* (J.D. Caputo, Ed.). New York: Fordham University Press.

Derrida, J. & Roudinesco, E. (2004). *For what tomorrow...A dialogue* (J. Fort, Trans.). Stanford, CA: Stanford University Press. (Original work published 2001).

Dunbar, Jr., C., Rodriguez, D., & Parker, L. (2002). Race, subjectivity, and the interview process. In J.F. Gubrium & J.A. Holstein (Eds.), *Handbook of interview research* (pp. 279–298). Thousand Oaks, CA: Sage Publications.

Dworkin, C. (2003). *Reading the illegible.* Evanston, IL: Northwestern University Press.

Dyer, R. (1988). White. *Screen. 29*(4), 44–64.

Eagleton, T. (1983). *Literary theory: An introduction.* Minneapolis: University of Minnesota Press.

Eco, U. (1998). *Serendipities: Language and lunacy.* San Diego: Harcourt Brace.

Ellsworth, E. (1997). Double binds of whiteness. In M. Fine, L. Weis, L.C. Powell, & L. Mun Wong (Eds.), *Off white: Readings on race, power, and society* (pp. 259–269). New York: Routledge.

Fontana, A. & Frey, J.H. (2000). The Interview: From structured questions to negotiated text. In N. K. Denzin & Y. S. Lincoln (Eds.), *Handbook of qualitative research* (2nd ed., pp. 645–672). Thousand Oaks, CA: Sage Publications.

Frankenberg, R. (1996). When we are capable of stopping, we begin to see. In B. Thompson & S. Tyagi (Eds.), *Names we call home: Autobiography on racial identity* (pp. 3–17). New York: Routledge.

———. (1993). *White women, race matters: The social construction of whiteness.* Minneapolis: University of Minnesota Press.

Frey, H.-J. (1996). *Studies in poetic discourse* (W. Whobrey, Trans.). Stanford, CA: Stanford University Press.

García, A.M. (2000). *Silence in the novels of Carmen Martin Gaíte.* New York: Peter Lang.

Garrison, J. (2004). Dewey, Derrida, and the 'double bind,' In P.P. Trifonas & M.A. Peters (Eds.), *Derrida, deconstruction and education: Ethics of pedagogy and research,* (pp. 95–108). Oxford, UK: Blackwell Publishing.

Geertz, C. (1973). *The interpretation of cultures.* New York: Basic Books.

Giroux, Henry A. (1988). *Teachers as intellectuals: Toward a critical pedagogy of learning.* New York: Bergin & Garvey.

Glesne, C. (1999). *Becoming qualitative researchers: An introduction* (2nd ed.). New York: Longman.

Greene, M. (1993). "The Passions of Pluralism: Multiculturalism and the Expanding Community," *Educational Researcher, 22*(1), 13–18.

Hass, R. (1996, September). *Poets on poetry.* Talk given at the Geraldine R. Dodge Poetry Festival, Waterloo, NJ.

Heidegger, M. (1962a). Being-there and discourse. Language. In *Being and time.* (pp. 203–211). J. Macquarrie & E. Robinson (Trans.). San Francisco, Harper & Row. (Original work published 1927).

———. (1962b). Idle-talk. In *Being and time.* (pp. 211–214). J. Macquarrie & E. Robinson (Trans.). San Francisco, Harper & Row. (Original work published 1927).

———. (1971). *On the way to language.* Peter D. Hertz (Trans.). San Francisco: HarperCollins. (Original work published 1959).

———. (1991). *The principle of reason.* Reginald Lilly (Trans.). Bloomington, IN: Indiana University Press. (Original work published 1957).

Holstein, J.A. & Gubrium, J.F. (1995). *The active interview.* Thousand Oaks, CA: Sage Publications.

Huberman, A.M. & Miles, M.B. (1994). Data management and analysis methods. In N. K. Denzin & Y. S. Lincoln (Eds.), *Handbook of qualitative research* (pp. 428–444). Thousand Oaks, CA: Sage Publications.

Hughes, L. (1994). Silence. In Arnold Rampersad (Ed.) & David Roessel (Assoc. Ed.), *The Collected Poems of Langston Hughes.* New York: Alfred A. Knopf.

Irigaray, L. (2002). *Between east and west: From singularity to community* (S. Pluháèek, Trans.). New York: Columbia University Press. (Original work published 1999).

Jackson, A.Y. (2006). *Fields of discourse: An analysis of schooling in a small, southern town.* Paper presented at the AERA Annual Meeting, April 2006, San Francisco, CA.

———. (2003). Rhizovacality. *Qualitative Studies in Education, 16*(5), 693-710.

Jaworski, A. (Ed.) (1997). *Silence: Interdisciplinary perspectives.* Berlin: Mouton de Gruyter.

———. (1993). *The power of silence: Social and pragmatic perspectives.* Newbury Park, CA: Sage Publications.

Johnson, B. (1981). Translators Preface in *Dissemination* by Jacques Derrida. London: The Athlone Press.

Jones, A. (1999). The limits of cross-cultural dialogue: Pedagogy, desire, and absolution in the classroom. *Educational Theory, 49*(3), 299–316.

Kelly, B. P. (1996, September). *Spoken poems and silent readings.* Talk given at the Geraldine R. Dodge Poetry Festival, Waterloo, NJ.

Kundera, M. (1984). *The unbearable lightness of being.* Michael Henry Heim (Trans.). New York: HarperCollins.

Kvale, S. (2006). Dominance through interviews and dialogues. *Qualitative Inquiry, 12*(3), 480–500.

———. (2006). *Interviewing between method and craft.* Paper presented at the AERA Annual Meeting, April 7, 2006, San Francisco, CA.

———. (1996). *InterViews: An introduction to qualitative research interviewing.* Thousand Oaks, CA: Sage.

Lakoff, G. & Johnson, M. (1980). *Metaphors we live by.* Chicago: The University of Chicago Press.

Lather, P. (forthcoming 2007) *Getting lost: Feminist efforts toward a double(d) science,* Albany NY: SUNY Press.

———. (2004). Applied Derrida: (Mis)Reading the work of mourning in educational research. In P.P. Trifonas & M.A. Peters (Eds.), *Derrida, deconstruction and education: Ethics of pedagogy and research* (pp. 3–16). Oxford, UK: Blackwell Publishing.

———. (2000). Reading the image of Rigoberta Menchú: Undecidability and language'lessons. *International Journal of Qualitative Studies in Education,* *13*(2), 153–162.

———. (1996). Troubling clarity: The politics of accessible language. *Harvard Educational Review, 66*(3), 525–545.

———. (1995). The validity of angels: Interpretive and textual strategies in researching the lives of women with HIV/AIDS. *Qualitative Inquiry, 1*(1), 41–68.

———. (1993). Fertile obsession: Validity after poststructuralism, *The Sociological Quarterly, 34*(4), 673–693.

Lather, P. & Smithies, C. (1997). *Troubling the angels: Women living with HIV/AIDS.* Boulder, CO: Westview Press.

LeCompte, M.D. & Preissle, J. (1993). *Ethnography and qualitative design in educational research* (2nd ed.). San Diego: Academic Press, Inc.

Lennard, J. (1996). *The poetry handbook: A guide to reading poetry for pleasure and practical criticism.* Oxford, UK: Oxford University Press.

Lewis, M. & Simon, R.I. (1986). A discourse not intended for her: Learning and teaching within patriarchy. *Harvard Educational Review, 56*(4), 457–472.

Li Li, H. (2004). Rethinking silencing silences. In Megan Boler (Ed.), *Democratic dialogue in education: Troubling speech, disturbing silence.* New York: Peter Lang.

Lincoln, Y.S. & Guba, E.G. (1985). *Naturalistic inquiry.* Newbury Park: Sage.

Lorde, A. (1984). *Sister outsider.* New York: Crossing Press.

Macbeth, D. (2001). On "reflexivity" in qualitative research: Two readings, and a third. *Qualitative Inquiry, 7*(1), 35–68.

MacClure, M. (2006). Remarks made as discussant in the session "Analysis and Representation: Poststructural Practices" at the AERA Annual Meeting, April 8, 2006, San Francisco, CA.

———. (2003). *Discourse* in *educational* and *social research.* Buckingham, UK: Open University Press.

Malabou, C. & Derrida, J. (2004). *Counterpath: Traveling with Jacques Derrida* (D. Wills, Trans.). Stanford, CA: Stanford University Press.

Mazzei, L.A. (2004). Silent listenings: Deconstructive practices in discourse-based research. *Educational Researcher, 33*(2), 26–34.

———. (2003). Inhabited silences: In pursuit of a muffled subtext. *Qualitative Inquiry, 9*(3), 355–368.

McCall, M.M. (2000). Performance ethnography: A brief history and some advice. In N. K. Denzin & Y. S. Lincoln (Eds.), *Handbook of qualitative research* (2nd ed., pp. 421–433). Thousand Oaks, CA: Sage Publications.

McGuire, P.C. (1985). *Speechless dialect: Shakespeare's open silences.* Berkeley, CA: University of California Press.

McIntosh, P. (1990). White privilege: Unpacking the invisible knapsack. *Independent School, 49*(2), 31–36.

Merleau-Ponty, M. (1964). *Signs.* (R.C. McCleary, Trans.). Evanston, IL: Northwestern University Press. (Original work published 1960).

Mishler, E.G. (1986). *Research interviewing: Context and narrative.* Cambridge, MA: Harvard University Press.

Morrison, T. (1992). *Playing in the dark: Whiteness and the literary imagination.* New York: Vintage Books.

Moyers, B. (1995). *The language of life: A festival of poets.* New York: Doubleday.

Nairn, K., Munro, J. & Smith, A.B. (2005). A counter-narrative of a 'failed' interview. *Qualitative Research, 5*(2), 221–244.

National Center for Education Statistics (2000). http://nces.ed.gov/pubs2000/100largest/table9.html

Ochs, E. (1979). Transcription as theory. In E. Ochs & B.B. Schieffelin (Eds.), *Developmental pragmatics* (pp. 43–72). New York: Academic Press, Inc.

Peters, M. (1999). (Posts-) modernism and structuralism: Affinities and theoretical innovations. *Sociological Research Online, 4* (3), http://www.socresonline.org.uk/socresonline/4/3/peters.html.

Peters, M.A. & Burbules, N.C. (2004). *Poststructuralism and educational research.* Lanham, MD: Rowman & Littlefield.

Picard, M. (1988). *The world of silence.* Washington, DC: Gateway Editions.

Piercy, M. (1991). Unlearning to not speak. In M. Sewell (Ed.), *Cries of the spirit* (p. 21). Boston: Beacon Press.

Pillow, W.S. (2003). Confessions, catharsis, or cure? Rethinking the uses of reflexivity as methodological power in qualitative research. *International Journal of Qualitative Studies in Education, 16* (2), 175–196.

———. (2002). When a man does feminism should he dress in drag? *International Journal of Qualitative Studies in Education, 15*(5), 545–554.

———. (2000). Deciphering attempts to decipher postmodern educational research. *Educational Researcher 29*(5), 21–24.

Reinharz, S. (1992). *Feminist methods in social research.* New York: Oxford University Press.

Rich, A. (1979). *On lies, secrets, and silence: Selected prose 1966-1978.* New York: W.W. Norton & Co.

———. (1993). *What is found there: Notebooks on poetry and politics.* New York: W.W. Norton & Company, Inc.

———. (1996). Defy the Space that Separates. *The Nation, 263*(10), 30-4.

Richardson, L. (1993). Poetics, dramatics, and transgressive validity. *The Sociological Quarterly, 34*(4), 695–710.

———. (1997). *Fields of play: Constructing an academic life.* New Brunswick, NJ: Rutgers University Press.

———. (2002). Poetic representation of interviews. In J.F. Gubrium & J.A. Holstein (Eds.), *Handbook of interview research* (pp. 877–891). Thousand Oaks, CA: Sage Publications.

Rosenberg, P.M. (1997). Underground discourses: Exploring whiteness in teacher education. In M. Fine, L. Weis, L.C. Powell, & L. Mun Wong (Eds.), *Off white: Readings on race, power, and society* (pp. 79–89). New York: Routledge.

Royle, N. (2000). What is deconstruction? In N. Royle (Ed.), *Deconstructions: A user's guide.* New York: Palgrave.

Rumi, J. (1995). *The essential Rumi* (C. Barks, Trans.). San Francisco: Harper.

Russel y Rodríguez, M. (1998). Confronting anthropology's silencing praxis: Speaking of/from a Chicana consciousness. *Qualitative Inquiry, 4*(1), 15–40.

Said, E. (1978). *Orientalism.* New York: Simon & Schuster.

St. Pierre, E.A. (2000). The call for intelligibility in postmodern educational research. *Educational Researcher, 29*(5), 25-28.

St. Pierre, E.A. (1997). Methodology in the fold and the irruption of transgressive data. *International Journal of Qualitative Studies in Education, 10*(2), 175-189.

St. Pierre, E.A. & Pillow, W.S., (Eds.), (2000). *Working the ruins: Feminist post structural theory and methods in education.* New York: Routledge.

Saville-Troike, M. (1985). The place of silence in an integrated theory of communication. In D. Tannen and M. Saville-Troike (Eds.) *Perspectives on Silence* (pp. 3–20). Norwood, NJ: Ablex Publishing Corporation.

Scheurich, J.J. (1997). *Research method in the postmodern.* London: RoutledgeFalmer.

———. (1995). A postmodernist critique of research interviewing. *International Journal of Qualitative Studies in Education, 8*(3), 239–252.

Schlant, E. (1999). *The language of silence: West German literature and the holocaust.* New York: Routledge.

Schneider, P. (1991). German postwar strategies of coming to terms with the past. In E. Schlant and J.T. Rimer (Eds.), *Legacies and ambiguities: Postwar fiction and culture in West Germany and Japan* (pp. 279–288). Baltimore: The Johns Hopkins University Press.

Schostak, J. (2006). *Interviewing and representation in qualitative research.* Berkshire, England: Open University Press.

Schrift, A.D. (1995). *Nietzsche's french legacy: A genealogy of poststructuralism.* New York: Routledge.

———. (1996). Nietzsche's french legacy. In B. Magnus and K. M. Higgins (Eds.), *The Cambridge companion to Nietzsche* (pp. 323–355). New York: Cambridge University Press.

Sontag, S. (1991). The aesthetics of silence. In *Styles of radical will.* New York: Anchor Books. (Original work published 1969).

Spivak, G.C. (1999) *A critique of postcolonial reason: Toward a history of the vanishing present.* Cambridge, MA: Harvard University Press.

———. (1976). Translator's Preface. In *Of Grammatology* by Jacque Derrida. Baltimore: The Johns Hopkins University Press.

Spivak, G. C. with Rooney, E. (1997). "In a word": Interview. In L. Nicholson (Ed.), *The second wave: A reader in feminist theory* (pp. 356–378). New York: Routledge. (Original work published 1989).

Stern, G. (1996, September). *Spoken poems and silent readings.* Talk given at the Geraldine R. Dodge Poetry Festival, Waterloo, NJ.

Strean, H. S. (1990). *Resolving resistances in psychotherapy.* New York: Bruner/Mazel Publishers.

Stronach, I. (2002). This space is not yet blank: Anthropologies for a future action research. *Educational Action Research, 10*(9), 291–307.

Stronach, I., Garratt, D., Pearce, C. & Piper, H. (forthcoming). Reflexivity, The picturing of selves, The forging of method. *Qualitative Inquiry.*

Stronach, I. & MacLure, M. (1997). *Educational research undone: The postmodern embrace.* Bristol, PA: Open University Press.

Tannen, D. (1989). *Talking voices: Repetition, dialogue and imagery in conversational discourse.* New York: Cambridge University Press.

Tannen D. & Saville-Troike M. (Eds.). (1985). *Perspectives on silence.* Norwood, NJ: Ablex Publishing Corporation.

Tavris, C. (1992). *The mismeasure of woman.* New York: Simon & Schuster.

Taylor, M.C. (1986). Introduction: System...Structure...Difference ...Other. In M. Taylor (Ed.). *Deconstruction in context: Literature and philosophy,* (pp. 1–34). Chicago: The University of Chicago Press.

Templeton, J.F. (1994). *The focus group: A strategic guide to organizing, conducting, and analyzing the focus group interview* (Rev. ed.). Chicago: Probus.

Trifonas, P.P. & Peters, M.A., (Eds.). (2004). *Derrida, deconstruction and education: ethics of pedagogy and research.* Oxford, UK: Blackwell.

U.S. Department of Education. (1997). *America's teachers: Profile of a profession, 1993-94.* http://nces.ed.gov/pubsearch/pubsinfo.asp?pubid=97460.

Van Maanen, J. (1988). *Tales of the field: On writing ethnography.* Chicago: University of Chicago Press.

Waller, A. (2006). The first time is always memorable. Paper presented at the AERA Annual Conference, San Francisco, CA, April 2006

Wood, D. (Ed.). (1992). *Derrida: A critical reader.* Cambridge, MA: Blackwell.

Wood, J. (2006). A Fresh View. In *The Guardian Review,* October 30, 2006, pp. 12–13.

Yoshino, K. (2006). The Pressure to Cover. In *The New York Times Magazine,* January 15, 2006, pp. 32–45, 62, 68, 72.

INDEX

Studies in the Postmodern Theory of Education

General Editors
Joe L. Kincheloe & Shirley R. Steinberg

Counterpoints publishes the most compelling and imaginative books being written in education today. Grounded on the theoretical advances in criticalism, feminism, and postmodernism in the last two decades of the twentieth century, Counterpoints engages the meaning of these innovations in various forms of educational expression. Committed to the proposition that theoretical literature should be accessible to a variety of audiences, the series insists that its authors avoid esoteric and jargonistic languages that transform educational scholarship into an elite discourse for the initiated. Scholarly work matters only to the degree it affects consciousness and practice at multiple sites. Counterpoints' editorial policy is based on these principles and the ability of scholars to break new ground, to open new conversations, to go where educators have never gone before.

For additional information about this series or for the submission of manuscripts, please contact:

Joe L. Kincheloe & Shirley R. Steinberg
c/o Peter Lang Publishing, Inc.
29 Broadway, 18th floor
New York, New York 10006

To order other books in this series, please contact our Customer Service Department:

(800) 770-LANG (within the U.S.)
(212) 647-7706 (outside the U.S.)
(212) 647-7707 FAX

Or browse online by series:
www.peterlang.com